CITYSPOTS
HAMB

Paul Murphy

Written by Paul Murphy; introductory texts by Trevor Salisbury
Updated by Debby Mayes

Published by Thomas Cook Publishing
A division of Thomas Cook Tour Operations Limited
Company registration No: 1450464 England
The Thomas Cook Business Park, 9 Coningsby Road
Peterborough PE3 8SB, United Kingdom
Email: books@thomascook.com, Tel: +44 (0)1733 416477
www.thomascookpublishing.com

Produced by The Content Works Ltd
Aston Court, Kingsmead Business Park, Frederick Place
High Wycombe, Bucks HP11 1LA
www.thecontentworks.com

Series design based on an original concept by Studio 183 Limited

ISBN: 978-1-84157-905-4

First edition © 2006 Thomas Cook Publishing
This second edition © 2008 Thomas Cook Publishing
Text © Thomas Cook Publishing
Maps © Thomas Cook Publishing/PCGraphics (UK) Limited
Transport map © Communicarta Limited

Series Editor: Kelly Anne Pipes
Production/DTP: Steven Collins

Printed and bound in Spain by GraphyCems

Cover photography (Rathaus Town Hall with statues of the city mascot
Hans Hummel) © David Sutherland/Alamy

CONTENTS

CITYSPOTS

SYMBOLS KEY

The following symbols are used throughout this book:

ⓐ address ⓣ telephone ⓕ fax ⓦ website address ⓔ email
ⓛ opening times ⓝ public transport connections ⓘ important

The following symbols are used on the maps:

ℹ️	information office	▨	points of interest
✈	airport	○	city
➕	hospital	○	large town
🛡	police station	○	small town
🚌	bus station	═	motorway
🚆	railway station	─	main road
Ⓤ	U-Bahn	─	minor road
Ⓢ	S-Bahn	─	railway
✝	cathedral		
❶	numbers denote featured cafés & restaurants		

Hotels and restaurants are graded by approximate price as follows:
£ budget price ££ mid-range price £££ expensive

◗ *Hamburg's busy docks seen from Landungsbrücken*

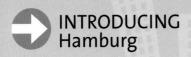

INTRODUCING
Hamburg

Introduction

What do you think of when you hear the name Hamburg? Red light districts, Reeperbahn, perhaps the Beatles, even? Or a grey, industrial monster dominated by factory chimneys and dreary docks? While Reeperbahn, football and anecdotes about the Beatles' formative years are important to the people of Hamburg, factory chimneys need not even feature in your stay.

The city has some very attractive neighbourhoods, and visitors are surprised at just how green it is, with its tree-lined streets and parks. What's more, there's a fascinating combination of historic and modern architecture.

The city is dominated by water, with the Alster lakes in the city centre, the River Elbe providing the harbour and any number of canals and waterways. There are beautiful bridges to discover (Hamburg boasts more than Venice), waterfront bars and cafés to enjoy and boat trips to take.

But back to the Reeperbahn: yes, there are prostitution, sex shops and peepshows, but music and dancing are by far the district's dominant influences.

In recent years Hamburg has really geared itself to welcoming tourists, opening trendy hotels, revamping museums and giving whole areas a complete facelift. The most obvious example is the dockland *Speicherstadt*, 20 years ago a collection of rapidly emptying warehouses, now home to many of Hamburg's most important tourist attractions. Up-and-coming areas just outside the city centre now offer an exciting array of home-grown fashion, cutting-edge music and ethnic cuisines. And if that doesn't whet your appetite, there's always the football...

○ *Nikolaifleet is one of Hamburg's many city-centre canals*

When to go

SEASONS & CLIMATE

Although the average temperature for the year only reaches 9.6°C (49°F), with 1.7°C (36°F) in January and 18.3°C (65°F) in July, these are only averages, and summer days can be much warmer (and winter days colder). The temperature in summer can certainly be high enough to cause sunburn, especially if you're spending time on or near the water.

Admittedly, it rains on average one day in every three in Hamburg but in summer, especially, you would be unlucky to be rained out more than a day, and in any case there's plenty to see and do in Hamburg on a wet day (see pages 46–7).

ANNUAL EVENTS

No matter what your interests are, you are certain to find an event to your taste. The following list represents only the most notable – there are plenty more of more specialist interest, which the Tourist Office and its website (see page 152) can provide information on.

March & April

Frühlingsfest Month-long fair on Heiligengeistfeld, St Pauli.
14 Mar–13 Apr 2008; 20 Mar–29 Apr 2009
Ⓦ www.hamburger–dom.de
Hamburg Marathon Starting and ending at the Hamburg Trade Fair grounds, coinciding with the Marathon & Running trade fair.
27 Apr 2008; 28 Apr 2009. Ⓦ www.marathon-hamburg.de (For details of the fair Ⓦ www.hamburg-messe.de)

May & June

Port's Anniversary Help Hamburg celebrate its anniversary (see below)

Tennis Masters Series, held in Rotherbaum just north of the city centre. 10–18 May 2008; exact dates in May 2009 to be announced
ⓦ www.dtb-tennis.de/AmRothenbaum

HAMBURG'S ANNIVERSARY

Hamburg celebrates the anniversary of its port every May with a huge gathering of ships, from yachts to stately clippers. A big anniversary (Hamburg has been a port for over 800 years) demands a big party, and the event regularly attracts over a million visitors. In 1189 Emperor Friedrich Barbarossa issued the citizens of Hamburg with a charter granting them an exemption from customs duties for their ships from the River Elbe to the North Sea, thereby opening Hamburg's gateway to the world. Highlights include a fireworks display and a special service in St Michaelis, the grand entrance parade to the port for all of the participating ships. Other items not to be missed are the tug ballet, in which tugboats actually dance along to music, and the dragon boat race.

On land it all happens along the *Hafenmeile* or 'Harbour mile' that stretches from the Speicherstadt to the fish market, providing space for food and entertainment for children and families. Fairground attractions are interspersed with souvenir stalls, bars and several stages offering live music from Gipsy Swing to rock. There's also a strong aerial element: visitors can float in a hot-air balloon, take a flight in a helicopter, watch parachuting or see how choppers are used to save lives. ◑ 9–12 May 2008, 8–10 May 2009 ⓦ www.hafengeburtstag.de

July & August

SchlagerMove Two-day 'Festival of Love' in St Pauli. Go back to the 60s and 70s and enjoy cheesy German pop music and a freaky party. The main event is on the second day, with a parade beginning at the Hamburger Dom park. 4 & 5 July 2008, 3 & 4 July 2009
Ⓦ www.schlagermove.de

Sommerdom Funfair (on the same site as the Frühlingsfest). 25 Jul–24 Aug 2008; 24 Jul–23 Aug 2009 Ⓦ www.hamburger-dom.de

Vattenfall-Cyclassics Annual open cycling event in July & August.
ⓘ (hotline) 0900 1877 6588 33 Ⓦ www.vattenfall-cyclassics.de

Alstervergnügen Binnenalster Gastro fair, live music and fireworks festival in late August, the whole way around the Alster Lake.
Ⓦ www.alstervergnuegen-hamburg.net

CityManTriathlon (at the end of August, exact dates to be announced).
ⓘ (040) 881 800 29 Ⓦ www.hamburgcityman@upsolut.de

○ *Many a festive fancy is available at the Christmas Markets*

September

Reeperbahn Festival Three days of rock, pop and indie played open-air on the Spielbudenplatz as well as in a plethora of clubs on and around the Reeperbahn. Tickets (available on-line) start at €26 for a one-day pass. Late September, exact dates to be announced.
ⓦ www.reeperbahnfestival.com

November & December

Tag der Kunstmeile (Day of the Art Mile) A mile of cultural centres and events to sample, almost for free, in late November (see pages 18–19).

Christmas Markets From the end of November up to Christmas Eve there is a historic Christmas market in front of the Rathaus (town hall) and six others at various sites around the city – for up-to-date details check ⓦ www.hamburg-tourism.de

Christmas Parade on the Mönckebergstrasse, 14.00–16.00 every Saturday in December.

PUBLIC HOLIDAYS
Neujahr (New Year's Day) 1 January
Karfreitag (Good Friday) 21 March 2008, 10 April 2009
Ostermontag (Easter Monday) 24 March 2008, 13 April 2009
Maifeiertag (Labour Day) 1 May
Himmelfahrt (Ascension Day) 1 May 2008; 21 May 2009
Pfingstmontag (Whit Monday) 12 May 2008; 1 June 2009
Tag der Deutschen Einheit (Day of Unification) 3 October
1 & 2 Weihnachtstage (Christmas Day & Boxing Day) 25 & 26 December

The Beatles in Hamburg

In 1960 John Lennon, Paul McCartney, George Harrison, Stu Sutcliffe (bass) and Pete Best (drums) were a fairly rough-and-ready band without a proper name who weren't getting many gigs in Liverpool. They were asked to go to Hamburg, where other Liverpool bands were popular, and jumped at the chance. 'The Reeperbahn and the Grosse Freiheit were the best things we'd ever seen', said George later. 'There were seedy things about it, obviously, including some of the conditions we had to live in when we first got there.'

The band first played at the Indra at 64 Grosse Freiheit (still there) and it was here that they adopted the name The Beatles. They lived just around the corner off the top of Grosse Freiheit at 33 Paul-Roosen Strasse in the Bambi Kino (cinema) – 'a pigsty' in John's words – this building's also still in existence. They moved from the Indra to the Kaiserkeller (see page 119), where they met Ringo, and stayed here until their work permit expired. The following year they returned to

Hamburg and played the Top Ten Club, at 136 Reeperbahn (still here, next to the Reeperbahn S-Bahn) and the Star Club, which was to be their most famous venue. In 1962 they returned to the Star Club three times, in January, November and December. Their last gig in Hamburg was 31 December 1962. The original Star Club burned down many years ago and only a plaque now marks the site where the Beatles, Jimmy (sic) Hendrix, Ray Charles, Gene Vincent, Bo Diddley and many other music legends played. You'll find it opposite the Kaiserkeller through an archway in a small courtyard.

For more on this seminal and fascinating period in the life of the Fab Four, buy the CD *The Savage Young Beatles in Hamburg 1961: A Musical Biography*, which is a first-hand account including reminiscences from most of the people who were there. There is also a guided walking tour, *The Beatles in St Pauli – a Magical Mystery Tour* (see box, page 112).

● *Grosse Freiheit's clubland is where the Beatles were born*

History

Hamburg's journey to the prominence and prosperity it enjoys today could be summed up in three words: triumph over adversity. From its first definite appearance as a fourth-century Saxon settlement, the city developed steadily over the centuries and became a key member of the Hanseatic League of German trading cities. This gave it a firm economic foundation, and things really took off half-way through the 19th century when the *Hamburg-Amerikanischen Packetfahrt-Aktien-Gesellschaft* ('HAPAG', thankfully) was founded and became the most important shipping line for emigrants to North America. HAPAG was a licence to print *Marks* and Hamburg looked to be sitting pretty for years to come. But two world wars in the next hundred years came very close to destroying the city, not only in terms of its urban infrastrucure and economy, but also of its population – indeed, over 40,000 of its civilians perished in World War II bombing raids. Even as the post-war rebuilding programme was coming to completion in 1962, major flooding caused by the worst storm in living memory killed 315 people and left more than 60,000 homeless.

The second half of the last century saw Hamburg sitting rather too close to the Iron Curtain for comfort, a fact that seems to have cramped its style in some ways; by far the biggest event in the city's recent history was the reunification of Germany in 1990. Before that, it was only possible to travel 50 km (31 miles) eastwards before hitting the border to the former DDR (German Democratic Republic). Once the Curtain was torn down, the people of Hamburg had access to a whole new recreation area along the Baltic coast and incorporating the lake district of Mecklenburg-Vorpommern. They also had new possibilities and, most importantly, new hope. The pace of life in the harbour has changed greatly over the years, with dock workers being replaced by technology as container shipping has become more and more important. More and more money is being generated, and the 1990s saw the beginning of work on *HafenCity*, one of Europe's most ambitious building projects (see page 91), transforming the hitherto neglected dockland area.

At the start of the 21st century, The Free and Hanseatic city of Hamburg (to give it its full name), is in great shape. In 2006 it acquitted itself splendidly as one of the host cities of the Football World Cup, thus raising both its profile and its self-confidence. Its tourism industry is the fastest-growing in Germany, its people are very probably the friendliest, and its future – if it manages to avoid the the calamity that has occasionally visited in the past – is full of possibilities.

⬥ *Hammonia, patron goddess of Hamburg*

Lifestyle

Hamburg is a cosmopolitan seaport and industrial centre of more than 1.7 million inhabitants. Like large ports everywhere, it has welcomed visitors of every culture and nationality for centuries and this has resulted in an outward-looking, tolerant and worldly-wise attitude among its citizens. The fact that it has a student population of over 60,000 helps keep the atmosphere lively, and around 15 per cent of Hamburg's population are immigrants, giving the city a cosmopolitan outlook.

Generally speaking, people in Hamburg are very friendly, making it easy to start a conversation with them, especially since English is the main foreign language in German schools. Nevertheless, social etiquette is a little more formal than British and North American visitors may be used to. It is normal, even among younger people, to shake hands when you meet and again when departing as a gesture of friendship.

Smoking is no longer allowed on public transport, in pubs, bars and restaurants, unless a completely separate room is available for smokers; it is, however, tolerated in beer tents.

Hamburg is famous for its nightlife – *In Hamburg sind die Nächte lang*, as the German saying goes ('In Hamburg the nights are long') – and the notoriety of parts of St Pauli, especially the Reeperbahn, is another legacy of the city's historic role as a home from home for the world's sailors. In fact Hamburg offers every kind of entertainment, from high-brow classical music and theatre to cutting-edge pop. A whole-hearted appetite for life characterises the people of this energetic city, belying the stereotype, common even in its home country, of the dour North German character. Like most Germans, Hamburgers are great 'joiners', belonging to large numbers of clubs and societies – not only the traditional sports clubs but associations for all interests, from allotment gardening to square dancing.

Hamburg is not only Germany's second-biggest city but also its undisputed media centre, home to most of Germany's largest newspaper and book publishing empires and over 17,000 companies in the realms of film, radio, TV and advertising.

◆ *A night in the pub is all the nightlife many Hamburgers want*

Culture

Hamburg has a lot to offer by way of culture. Theatres, museums, musical theatres and concerts: it's all there.

Visitors who would like to know more about the history of Hamburg and life in bygone times could visit one of the almost 90 museums and collections. Here you are certain to find something which interests you. These include a wine museum, a museum dedicated to Johannes Brahms, a museum for Hamburg's history, one for ethnology, two museum ships and a museum submarine. Even Ohlsdorf Cemetery has a museum, and if none of this interests you, you can always try the Erotic Art Museum (see page 112), which interests everybody.

You have just as wide a choice if you are a theatre-goer. Hamburg is home to no less than 34 theatres, offering everything from cabaret to puppet shows. It doesn't matter if you don't speak German – the English Theatre stages plays in English, from Shakespeare to Pinter and even Noel Coward – between September and June (see page 28). If you are around in September you can sample the whole gamut of Hamburg drama in the Long Theatre Night, when you have the opportunity of popping in and out of a variety of performances.

Hamburg is also big on musicals – the *The Lion King* even has its own theatre in the harbour. Concerts abound throughout the year at venues ranging from churches to the **Color Line Arena** (ⓦ www.colorline-arena.com) and the **Congress Centre** (ⓦ www.hamburg-messe.de).

A highlight of the Hamburg cultural calendar has to be the Tag der Kunstmeile (Day of the Art Mile). On this day (ⓦ www.hamburg.de/behoerden/museen/kmh), the Kunsthalle (Arts Hall), the Museum für Kunst und Gewerbe (Arts and Trade Museum), the Galerienhaus

(Gallery House), the Kunsthaus (House of Art), the Kunstverein (Art Association), the Freie Akademie der Künste (Free Academy of the Arts) the Deichtor halls, Galerie 1 of the Hamburg Savings Bank (Haspa) and the Zentralbibliothek (central library), which are all situated along the 1.5 km (1 mile) route between the Alster and the Harbour, invite visitors to come in and take a look around between 10.00 and 24.00. Performances, concerts, short guided tours of the premises

⬇ *Modern architecture housing modern art – Galerie der Gegenwart*

Evening light show in Planten un Blomen park

and a party are all on offer. The visitors also do not have to worry about getting back either, as shuttle buses are provided every half hour between 11 am and midnight.

Above all, culture is seen as fun in Hamburg – and hardly an event is staged which doesn't involve a closing party. The range of cultural attractions is so wide that you need to narrow it down a little and check out what's happening when you are due to visit: make the Tourist Office or its website your first stop (see page 152).

Typical Hamburg – waterways and spires

Shopping

As befits one of the world's greatest historical trading centres, Hamburg can be one long purchasing spree. The main shopping street is Mönckebergstrasse, near the central railway station. There are many fashion outlets, such as Benetton or Esprit, while funky homegrown clobber can be found in the Karolinenviertel and Schanzenviertel neighbourhoods north of the city centre (see page 105). Look out for reasonably-priced CDs and DVDs in the megastores at the main stations (Saturn, Mediamarkt) – they're much cheaper than at home.

There are more than ten shopping centres, one of which, the Europa Passage (round the corner from the Rathaus, see page 76), is home to the well-stocked English section at the Thalia bookshop.

Despite its name, you can buy almost anything at the Sunday Fischmarkt (Fish Market, see page 114) in St Pauli – as well as fish, of course.

Bright and colourful weekly markets selling fresh produce from local farms are featured in every Hamburg neighbourhood. Try the **Hopfenmarkt** near the Speicherstadt (🕙 11.00–16.00 Tues & Thurs), or Hamburg's favourite and most colourful market, **Isemarkt** (🕙 Tues & Fri mornings 🚇 U-bahn: U3 to Hoheluftbrücke or Eppendorfer Baum).

The **Flohcampus** flea market is held at the university's Von-Melle-Park (🕙 08.00–16.00 Sat 🚌 Bus: 4, 5 to Grindelhof). Summer Saturdays see an arts and antiques market on the Spielbudenplatz/Reeperbahn, while on winter weekends there's a huge indoor antiques and flea market at the Congress Centre.

Souvenir stalls abound, whether on the Rathaus square or down at the harbour. If you'd like to take home a Hamburg flag, you might like to browse in the **Fahnenfleck** shop (🏠 Neuer Wall 57 ☎ (040) 320 85 770). Not only are they official suppliers of all the city's flags,

USEFUL SHOPPING PHRASES

What time do the shops open/close?
Um wieviel Uhr öffnen/schliessen die Geschäfte?
Oom veefeel oor erffnen/shleessen dee geshefter?

How much is this?
Wieviel kostet das?
Veefeel kostet das?

Can I try this on?
Kann ich das anprobieren?
Can ikh das anprobeeren?

My size is ...
Ich habe Grösse ...
Ikh haber grerser ...

I'll take this one, thank you
Ich nehme das, danke schön
Ikh neymer das, danker shern

Can you show me the one in the window/that one?
Zeigen Sie mir bitte das im Fenster/dieses da?
Tsyegen zee mere bitter dass im fenster/deezess da?

they have a wonderful selection of fancy-dress accessories. Shopping for German food, wine and beer is a delight, whether at a specialist *Delikatessen* or in the food halls of the big stores. Sample German wines before deciding which bottle(s) to buy at Bocksbeutel in den Colonnaden (see page 79). Tea is very popular in Hamburg: look out for cosy little shops in all parts of town selling an unbelievable assortment, particularly scented teas. **Tea Embassy** (③ Grosse Bleichen 12–4 ① (040) 30 70 99 43) is worth visiting for the shop interior alone, all dark wood and crystal chandeliers and absolutely charming service.

Eating & drinking

Hamburg rightly claims to be the gastronomic capital of Germany. It's not surprising that a place that's been the country's gateway to the world for centuries should offer a vast range of national cuisines, or that its media capital should boast some superb restaurants.

First, let's clarify what a venue's title may suggest. Here, an establishment calling itself a *restaurant* is likely to be fairly upmarket; more traditional places will be a *Gasthof* or *Gaststätte*. For simpler food, try a *Brauhaus* (where the range and quality of the beers are actually paramount), a *Kneipe* (a pub), a café or a bistro. Wherever you go, hygiene, service and portions are likely to be impressive, though bear in mind that the more modest establishments may not take credit cards.

If all you want is coffee and cake, you can drop in not only to a café but also at almost any bakery (*Bäckerei*), where you can choose from a delicious range of cakes (*Kuchen*) or filled tarts (*Törtchen*) and eat them at a table as you sip your coffee.

Naturally, Hamburg makes much of its fish dishes, such as *Hamburger Pannfisch mit Bratkartoffeln* (German fish and chips). Eel (*Aal*) dishes are popular, and you will often find *Hamburger Aalsuppe* on the menu. This might not be eel soup – often the *Aal* stands for 'all', as in 'all manner of ingredients'. *Labskaus*, a kind of seaman's hash, contains corned beef and herring with mashed

RESTAURANT PRICE CATEGORIES
Ratings used in the book are based on the average cost per person of a three-course meal, without drinks.
£ up to €25   ££ €25–35   £££ over €35

potatoes and beetroot, often topped with a fried egg. Do try *Rote Grütze* – it's a North German dessert made from red berries and served with custard or cream.

If you hunger for the products of Pizza Hut and McDonalds, you'll find them in Hamburg: they'll taste exactly like the ones back home. Local alternatives for cheap eats are the 12 *Nordsee* fish restaurants scattered around the city, where you can either eat in or take away at prices starting at around €5. The *Schweinske* restaurants also offer an excellent range of pork dishes, all under €10, alongside Germany's most popular fast food, *Currywurst* – a frankfurter-style sausage in a curry sauce. Actually, the food in most pubs and local restaurants is far from expensive, and visitors on a budget are unlikely to leave Hamburg hungry or starved of choice.

The cosmopolitan population means it's easy to find ethnic cuisines of all kinds. Little Turkish snack bars are everywhere, selling kebabs and *börek*, and Asian snack bars and restaurants are increasingly

● *Think Hamburg, think seafood, think Omega 3 food*

popular, particularly in the trendier neighbourhoods like Schanzenviertel. The area between Landungsbrücken and Baumwall stations boasts a concentration of Spanish and Portuguese bars and restaurants, while Greek, Italian and Chinese restaurants are scattered throughout the town. For Japanese food, particularly sushi, try the area around the Opera House.

Vegetarians traditionally have had a hard time finding places to eat in meat-loving Germany, but there's usually no trouble locating vegetarian options in Chinese, Thai or Indian restaurants. Even more locally inspired restaurants are vegging up, and most places will do a decent salad or pasta meal. As vegetarianism has become ever-more popular, so many German vegetarian restaurants have become more mainstream: check out Café Koppel on the Lange Reihe in St Georg (see page 79) or Schanzenstern (Schanzenviertel) at luchtime for exclusively vegetarian menus (see page 106). Alternatively, try the excellent **Boussi Falafel** takeaway downstairs in the Europa Passage.

One of the benefits of the amount of green space within the city is the opportunity it gives for a do-it-yourself lunch – or even a barbecue. Favourite places include the Alster Lake north of the city centre (see pages 60–4), the Planten un Blomen Park (see page 104), the beach beyond Övelgönne (see page 114) and even the yacht harbour in Wedel. The most inexpensive places to buy food for a picnic are discount grocery stores such as Lidl, Aldi or Plus, or at one of the farmers' markets (see page 22). You often find market stalls dedicated to a variety of salads, ranging from potato salad and coleslaw, through egg salad to fish-based salads (herring or shrimp). Ready-to-eat dishes can be obtained at specialist delicatessens and the food departments of large department stores, which are always of a very high standard. Filled rolls can be bought at any bakery, and all major stations house outlets such as **Mr.Clou**, selling sandwiches, wraps, salads and freshly pressed juices.

USEFUL DINING PHRASES

I would like a table for ... people
Ein Tisch für ... Personen, bitte
Ine teesh foor ... perzohnen, bitter

Waiter/waitress!
Herr Ober/Fräulein, bitte!
Hair ohber/froyline, bitter!

May I have the bill, please?
Die Rechnung, bitte!
Dee rekhnung, bitter!

Could I have it well-cooked/medium/rare please?
Ich möchte es bitte durch/halb durch/englisch gebraten
Ikh merkhter es bitter doorkh/halb doorkh/eng-lish gebrarten

I am a vegetarian. Does this contain meat?
Ich bin Vegetarier/in (masc./fem.). Ist da Fleisch drin?
Ish bin veggetaareer/veggetaareerin. Isst dah flyshe drinn?

Where is the toilet (restroom) please?
Wo sind die Toiletten?
Voo zeent dee toletten?

I would like a cup of/two cups of/another coffee/tea, please
Eine Tasse/Zwei Tassen/noch eine Tasse Kaffee/Tee, bitte
Ikh merkhter iner tasser/tsvy tassen kafey/tey, bitter

I would like a beer/two beers, please
Ein Bier/Zwei Bier, bitte
Ine beer/tsvy beer, bitter

Entertainment & nightlife

You bet Hamburg's a night-time kind of place, and at the last count the city could offer three casinos, plus bars, clubs, and discos galore, not to mention cinemas, theatres and the hundreds of restaurants, local pubs and cafés. Most of this nightlife is concentrated in the city centre and the St Pauli or Schanzenviertel districts.

A lively English-language theatre scene is centered around the long-established **English Theatre** (ⓐ Lerchenfeld 14 ❶ (040) 227 7089), but if you like things a little more organic, a good bet's the **Irish Rover** pub, which stages readings and plays by the Rover Rep Theatre in its Celtic cellar (ⓐ Grossneumarkt 8 ❶ (040) 357 146 63).

Visitors who prefer to go to an opera or watch a ballet are catered for at the **Hamburg State Opera** and **Hamburg Ballet**, both of international class and housed in a common venue.

◗ Popular nightlife includes drinking in outdoor bars

WHAT'S ON

Pick up a free copy of *Hamburg: Pur* from the tourist office for all nightlife listings or buy the monthly *Szene* magazine from a newsagent. Both publications are in German only but it's easy to work out what's happening where. *Szene* also reviews places to eat and drink (Ⓦ www.szene-hamburg-online.de).

English-language cinema and theatre links can be found at Ⓦ www.englishpages.de.

Ⓦ www.bartime.de provides information on all the bars and even awards ratings for them.

Bookings can be made on-line or by phone, or from one of the 25 ticket agencies around Hamburg. Tickets for same-evening performance are available from the box office 90 minutes before curtain up (❸ Grosse Theaterstrasse 25; box office opera ❶ (040) 35 66 68; box office ballet ❶ (040) 35 68 68).

Dance clubs rotate from venue to venue, so don't be surprised to hear a different style of music if you return to a particular location.

The epicentre of the Hamburg bar and club scene is Grosse Freiheit, in the heart of St Pauli, but other streets to browse include the Spielbudenplatz and, of course, the Reeperbahn. Outside St Pauli the pace of nightlife is perhaps not quite so hot, but there are still plenty of options in the city centre and the Schanzenviertel, lying strategically between St Pauli and the University area.

Although most films are dubbed into German, you can watch the latest releases in English at **Grindel UFA,** in the University Quarter (❸ Grindelberg 7a ❶ (040) 449 333). Their party-atmosphere 'sneak preview' on Monday evenings at 20.00 is particularly recommended.

Sport & relaxation

SPECTATOR SPORTS

Football is probably Hamburg's number one spectator sport, and
Hamburg SV has long been one of the Bundesliga's top teams.
Home games are played, usually on Saturday afternoons, at the
55,000-seater **HSH Nordbank Arena** (Ⓝ S-bahn: S21 to Stellingen,
then bus shuttle). Hamburg SV Tickets can be obtained at the
HSV City Store (Ⓢ Schmiedestrasse 2, Ⓣ (hotline) 01805 478 478).

The last week of June sees a great week of horse-racing at the
track in the easterly neighbourhood **Horn**, culminating in the **German
Derby** on the first Sunday of July. Tickets start at €5. Ⓝ U-bahn: U3 to
Horner Rennbahn

Water sports can be witnessed everywhere you turn.

PARTICIPATION SPORTS

The **Hamburg Nordic Walking Park** in Alstertal offers ten different
routes of varying levels of difficulty. Start from Wellingsbüttel
Gatehouse (ⓃS-bahn: S1, S11 to Wellingsbüttel) and enjoy the landscape.
Or join Hamburg's students, managers and movers and go jogging
round the Alster Lake (7.5 km or 4.7 miles). Boat hire is available on
both banks of the Alster, either directly in front of the Hotel Atlantic
Kempinski, or at the Alte Rabenstrasse landing stage (rowing boats,
paddle boats; sailing boats only with appropriate licence).

RELAXATION

A good way of relaxing is to visit one of the 11 spas situated around
the city, inluding the ultimate in pampering at the Hotel Atlantic
Kempinski (see pages 36–7). Hamburg Tourism (see page 152) also
offer wellness packages at the city's hotels. If your hotel does not offer

health facilities, you might like to try the **Alsterschwimmhalle**, Hamburg's most central swimming baths with fitness area and sauna (women only on Tuesdays). Swimming starts at €5.20, sauna (incl. swimming) €14.50 ❸ Sechslingspforte ❶ (040) 18 88 90 Ⓦ www.baderland.de ❶ 06.30–23.00 Mon–Fri, 08.00–23.00 Sat & Sun Ⓝ U-bahn: U1 to Lübecker Strasse

◐ *The HSH Nordbank Arena – home to top league football*

Accommodation

Being a major trade and congress centre, the city's accommodation is skewed to the more expensive end of the market, but Hamburg still offers something for all pockets. Breakfast is seldom included in your room rate.

HOTELS

Hotel Schanzenstern £ Eco-hotel right in the middle of trendy Schanzenviertel, just to the north of the city centre. Single- to five-bed rooms avalaible, but none with TV or telephone. Rainwater system for bathroom facilities, all food served in the excellent in-house restaurant is certified organic and locally grown whenever possible. Sister house in Altona. ❸ Bartelsstrasse 12 ❶ (040) 43 29 04 09 ⓦ www.schanzenstern.de ❷ info@schanzenstern.de ❷ S-bahn: S21 S31; U-bahn: U3 to Sternschanze

Rock'n'Roll Hotel Kogge £ Originally founded for musicians and open-minded travellers, this tiny hotel slap bang in the middle of the party scene offers single and double rooms with themes ranging from Bollywood to Punk. The in-house bar sees DJ action

PRICE RATINGS
Hotels in Germany are graded according to a voluntary one–five star rating system, which conforms to international standards. The ratings in this book are based on the average price for a double room (breakfast not included), per night, as follows:
£ up to €60 **££** €60–140 **£££** over €140

most nights ⓐ Bernhard-Nocht-Strasse 59 ⓣ (040) 312872
ⓦ www.kogge-hamburg.de ⓔ info@kogge-hamburg.com
Ⓝ S-bahn: S1, S3 to Reeperbahn

25 Hours Hotel ££ Designed in the style of the 60s and 70s and
self–consciously cool, situated in Altona. Stages lots of rock and
pop events and parties... ⓐ Paul-Dessau-Strasse 2 ⓣ (040) 85 50 70
ⓦ www.25hours-hotel.com ⓔ info@25hours-hotel.com Ⓝ S-bahn:
S1, S11 to Bahrenfeld

Auto-Parkhotel Hamburg ££ In a quiet location but still close
to Reeperbahn and a short walk from the Fischmarkt. On-site
parking. ⓐ Lincolnstrasse 8 ⓣ (040) 31 00 24 ⓦ www.auto-
parkhotel-hamburg.de ⓔ info@auto-parkhotel-hamburg.de
Ⓝ S-bahn: S1, S3 to Reeperbahn

Fritzhotel ££ Seventeen rooms, all with different designs. The hip
Schanzen District starts on the doorstep. ⓐ Schanzenstrasse 101–103
ⓣ (040) 82 22 28 30 ⓦ www.fritzhotel.com ⓔ info@fritzhotel.com
Ⓝ U-bahn: U3; S-bahn: S21, S31 to Sternschanze

Hotel Boston ££ Young designer hotel in Schanzenviertel,
well-positioned for both city centre and harbour or St Pauli.
Lounge area with open fire, excellent in-house restaurant.
ⓐ Missundestrasse 2 ⓣ (040) 589 666 700 ⓦ www.boston-
hamburg.de ⓔ info@boston–hamburg.de Ⓝ S-bahn: S21, S31
to Holstenstrasse

Hotel Fürst Bismarck ££ Situated opposite the main railway station,
close to the Schauspielhaus and Kunsthalle. ⓐ Kirchenallee 46–49

☎ (040) 28 01 09 1 ⓦ www.fuerstbismarck.de
ⓔ hotel@fuerstbismarck.de ⓝ all lines to Hauptbahnhof

Hotel Graf Moltke Hamburg ££ Centrally located in St Georg,
close to the Alster Lake, museums, the theatre and shopping
passages. ⓐ Steindamm 1 ☎ (040) 28 01 15 4 ⓦ www.hotel-graf-
moltke.de ⓔ info@hotel-graf-moltke.de ⓝ all lines to Hauptbahnhof

Hotel Hanseatin ££ The only Hamburg hotel which solely accepts
female guests (also children up to the age of seven). Situated near the
Laeiszhalle concert hall and a walkable distance from the Congress
Centre. ⓐ Dragonerstall 11 ☎ (040) 34 13 45 ⓦ www.hotel-hanseatin.de
ⓔ frauen@hotel-hanseatin.de ⓝ U-bahn: U2 to Gänsemarkt

Hotel Norddeutscher Hof ££ Centrally situated, only a few hundred
metres from the railway station. ⓐ Kirchenallee 24 ☎ (040) 24 56 10
ⓦ www.hotel-norddeutscher-hof.de ⓔ hotel-norddeutscher-hof@
t-online.de ⓝ all lines to Hauptbahnhof

Hotel St Annen ££ A few minutes from the Port, Fischmarkt and
Reeperbahn on foot, and from the city centre by U-Bahn. Has a garden
terrace. ⓐ Annenstrasse 5 ☎ (040) 31 77 13 0 ⓦ www.hotelstannen.de
ⓔ info@hotelstannen.de ⓝ U-bahn: U3 to St Pauli

Hotel Wedina ££ The novelty here is that the hotel has a strong
literary bias and works in close association with the nearby Literatur
Haus. The list of well-known authors who have stayed here is endless,
and the hotel library boasts a signed copy of every book presented
at Literatur Haus readings. ⓐ Gurlittstrasse 23 ☎ (040) 28 08 90 0
ⓦ www.wedina.de ⓔ info@wedina.de ⓝ all lines to Hauptbahnhof

Ibis Hamburg St Pauli Messe ££ The formula behind this popular chain is good value without being in the least exciting or different. There are other Ibis hotels at the aiport and near the main station. ⓐ Simon-von-Utrecht-Strasse 63 ⓣ (040) 65 04 60 ⓕ (040) 65 04 65 55 ⓦ www.ibishotel.com ⓝ U-bahn: U3 to St Pauli

Junges Hotel ££ 135-room hotel situated close to the main railway station. Has a sauna, solarium and roof terrace. Excellent in-house bistro. ⓐ Kurt-Schumacher-Allee 14 ⓣ (040) 41 92 30 ⓦ www.junges–hotel.de ⓝ all lines to Hauptbahnhof

Ökotel Hamburg ££ What's an eco-hotel? One where all the room furnishings are of natural material, all the food served is from biologically cultivated ingredients and accompanied by bio-wine and eco-beer. The promise is 'an ecological lifestyle without foregoing comfort'. Situated in Schnelsen, a good 45 minutes from the city centre on public transport. ⓐ Holsteiner Chaussee 347 ⓣ (040) 55 97 30 0 ⓦ www.oekotel.de ⓔ info@oekotel.de ⓝ U-bahn: U2 to Niendorf Markt, then Bus: 191 to Scheelring

Stadhaushotel Hamburg ££ Convenient for the for city centre, harbour and St Pauli areas, this hotel is not only geared to the needs of disabled guests, but also employs staff with disabilities. On-site parking, garden terrace, quiet and airy rooms. Breakfast included in room rate. Able-bodied guests equally welcome! ⓐ Holstenstrasse 118 ⓣ (040) 38 99 200 ⓦ www.stadthaushotel.com ⓔ zufrieden@ stadthotel.com ⓝ Bus: 20, 115, 183, 283 to Max–Brauer–Allee Mitte

YoHo ££ Despite being marketed towards younger visitors, this is no cheap hostel. It offers 30 fairly luxurious rooms in a modernised villa on the outskirts of the fashionable Schanzenviertel. Pricing is according to age, and under-27s get a better deal. ⓐ Moorkamp 5 ⓣ (040) 28 41 910 ⓦ www.yoho-hamburg.de ⓔ yoho@yoho-hamburg.de ⓝ U-bahn: U2 to Christuskirche

East £££ Ultra-stylish, orientally-themed hotel in St Pauli, one block north of the Reeperbahn. State-of-the-art wellness centre, fine oriental cuisine. ⓐ Simon-von-Utrecht-Strasse 31 ⓣ (040) 30 99 30 ⓦ www.east-hamburg.de ⓔ info@east-hamburg.de ⓝ U-bahn: U3 to St Pauli

Empire Riverside Hotel £££ The height of comfort, this wonder of modern architecture towering above the harbour offers floor-to-ceiling panorama windows in all rooms. A further highlight is the 20up Lounge on the top floor. ⓐ Bernhard-Nocht-Strasse 97 ⓣ (040) 31 113 70 750 ⓦ www.empire-riverside.de ⓔ empire@hotel-hamburg.de ⓝ S-bahn: S1, S3; U-bahn: U3 to Landungsbrücken

Fairmont Vier Jahreszeiten £££ Hamburg's belle époque queen of hotels on the banks of the Binnenalster. Very central, very luxurious. ⓐ Neuer Jungfernstieg 9–14 ⓣ 040 34 94 0 ⓦ www.hvj.de ⓔ reservations.hvj@fairmont.de ⓝ all lines to Jungfernstieg

Hotel Atlantic Kempinski Hamburg £££ This Grand Hotel, opened in 1909, is a Hamburg landmark and enjoys the perfect city-centre setting, right on the Binnenalster Lake. It was made famous by James Bond (then Pierce Brosnan) who clambered over its roof in *Tomorrow Never Dies*. The old-world glamour of its high-ceilinged stuccoed rooms is complemented by modern efficiency and superb restaurants. ⓐ An der Alster 72–79 ⓣ (040) 28 880

◔ *The rather grand Hotel Atlantic*

ⓦ www.atlantic.de ⓔ hotel.atlantic@kempinski.com
Ⓝ all lines to Hauptbahnhof

Hotel Elysee £££ A short walk from the centre, this privately owned
five-star luxury hotel caters mostly for business people but is cheerful,
bright and lively and the staff are friendly and efficient. Rooms are
attractive and very comfortable and facilities include a brand new
Wellness Centre. ⓐ Rothenbaumchaussee 10 ⓣ (040) 41 41 20
ⓦ www.elysee.de ⓔ info@elysee.de Ⓝ S-Bahn: S21, S31 to Dammtor

Hotel Hafen Hamburg £££ In a perfect position for harbour-watching,
this landmark hotel towers above the Landungsbrücken. It is a mix
of old and new, with several different styles and sizes of room, so
choose carefully but do try to get a room at the front! Non-residents
can enjoy great views from its Restaurant Port and its Tower Bar

(see page 98). 🅐 Seewartenstrasse 9 🅣 (040) 31 11 30 🅦 www.hotel-hamburg.de 🅔 info@hotel-hamburg.de 🅝 S-bahn: S1, S3; U-bahn: U3 to Landungsbrücken

Hotel Louis C Jacobs £££ One of the 'Leading Small Hotels of the World'. Guests come here to experience the discreet lifestyle of a Hanseatic shipping magnate in some of Germany's most luxurious suites and rooms. It is set a little way out of town on the beautiful Elbchaussee near Blankenese and enjoys wonderful views from its linden-shaded terrace. The food is exceptional, the service perfect. 🅐 Elbchaussee 401–403 🅣 (040) 822 550 🅦 www.hotel-jacob.de 🅔 jacob@hotel-jacob.de 🅝 S-bahn: S1, S11 to Hochkamp; Bus: 36 to Sieberlingstrasse

Hotel Side £££ Cool and trendy with arty, 60s-influenced minimalist public areas, beautiful designer bedrooms and superb health facilities, this city-centre hotel is a paragon of early 21st-century style and efficiency. First-class service from a young, confident staff. Their Fusion bar restaurant offers excellent east-meets-west cuisine. 🅐 Drehbahn 49 🅣 (040) 30 99 90 🅦 www.side-hamburg.de 🅔 info@side-hamburg.de 🅝 U-bahn: U1 to Stephansplatz; U2 to Gänsemarkt

Mövenpick Hotel Hamburg £££ Fascinatingly situated in a 19th-century water tower in the middle of the popular Schanzenpark, the hotel boasts spectacular views from its 17 floors. Wellness area including sauna and solarium, restaurant, terrace and the Cave bar down in the vaults. 🅐 Schanzenstern 6 🅣 (040) 33 44 110 🅦 www.moevenpick.de 🅔 hotelhamburg@moevenpick.de 🅝 U-bahn: U3; S-bahn: S21, S31 to Sternschanze

YOUTH HOSTELS

Auf dem Stintfang Youth Hostel £ This hostel offers two- to eight-bed rooms and has a magnificent view of the port of Hamburg. Open to members of the International Youth Hostel Federation only. 🅰 Alfred-Wegener-Weg 5 ☎ (040) 313488 🆆 www.djh.de 🄴 jh-stintfang@djh.de 🅽 U-bahn: U3; S-bahn: S1, S3 to Landungsbrücken

Horner Rennbahn £ Offers two- to six-bed rooms, is next to a racecourse and just five U-Bahn stops from the city centre. Open to members of the International Youth Hostel Federation only. 🅰 Rennbahnstrasse 100 ☎ (040) 65 11 671 🆆 www.djh.de 🄴 jh-hamburghorn@djh.de 🅽 U-bahn: U3 to Horner Rennbahn

CAMPSITES

Camping Buchholz £ Forty spaces, for caravans and tents, in a residential area with fast connections to the city. Open all year. Bed & breakfast also available. 🅰 Kieler Strasse 374 ☎ (040) 540 45 32 🆆 www.camping-buchholz.de 🄴 info@camping-bucholz.de 🅽 Bus: 4 to Basselweg

Schnelsen-Nord £ A well-equipped site offering 145 spaces for tents and caravans, close to a large Swedish furniture store and not too far from the airport. 🅰 Wunderbrunnen 2 ☎ (040) 559 42 25 🆆 www.campingplatz-hamburg.de 🄴 service@campingplatz-hamburg.de 🅽 Bus: 191 to Dornröschenweg; Bus: 284 to Wunderbrunnen

THE BEST OF HAMBURG

Whether you're attracted to waterways and bridges, interested in architecture, a party person or an arts afficionado – Hamburg has something to entertain you.

TOP 10 ATTRACTIONS

- **Spend a night in St Pauli** It's tacky, fun for many and offensive to some. You haven't seen Hamburg until you've been here (see pages 115–20).

- **Harbour Tour** Hamburg owes its prosperity to its maritime trade, and making a trip around the harbour essential. The scale alone is impressive (see page 91).

- **Cruise on the Alster Lake** Take an Alster-Kreuz-Fahrt on a sunny day. Hop off to visit fashionable lakeside cafés or to picnic in the Alsterpark (see page 64).

- **Museum für Hamburgische Geschichte (Hamburg History Museum)** One of your best options for a rainy day, the museum is very informative and all exhibits have English captions (see pages 67–8).

- **Take in a jazz session** Hamburg is known for its jazz scene, so be part of the appreciative audience in a crowded little bar.

- **Fischmarkt (Sunday Fish Market)** Even non-German speakers will smile at the banter at this lively weekly event. Live music, souvenirs and great food bargains (see page 114).

- **Speicherstadt** The world's biggest warehouse complex: historical urban architecture and enough attractions to warrant putting it on your A-list (see pages 94–5).

- **Michaeliskirche** Three-organ concert at noon, fantastic views over the port from the tower and 17th-century almshouses right next door (see page 66).

- **Blankenese**, for its hilly Treppenviertel (Staircase Quarter), messing about on the beach and finishing the day in a cosy thatched tearoom (see pages 124–9).

- **Lübeck** Make time for a day out to this beautiful, well-preserved historic city, less than an hour's train ride from Hamburg (see pages 130–42).

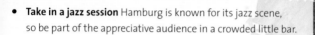
▼ *Enjoy a quiet coffee at the foot of this statue, behind the town hall*

Suggested itineraries

HALF-DAY: HAMBURG IN A HURRY

Go to the lakeside at Jungfernstieg and take a one-hour tour of the picturesque Alster Lake. The views back to the city centre are excellent and you will get a commentary, not only about the Alster and its grand houses, but about the city, too. Back on shore, take the U-Bahn U3 from Jungfernstieg station to Landungsbrücken, where you have a panoramic view of the docks. Take a walk along the front on the floating landing stages, grabbing a fish sandwich en route. From here you can go back to Jungfernstieg for shopping, or continue the maritime theme by visiting the *Rickmer-Rickmers* or *Cap San Diego* museum ships.

1 DAY: TIME TO SEE A LITTLE MORE

If you would rather see big ships than big houses, take a harbour tour instead of the lake tour, then drive round the Alster on a one-hour bus tour. Both depart from the Landungsbrücken, so you can step from one straight to the other. While you are at the docks, however, you may wish to make the short detour (ten-minute walk) to Deichstrasse to see Hamburg's oldest surviving buildings, where you can also get lunch, then cross the river to the Speicherstadt warehouse complex, where the Spice Museum is recommended.

2–3 DAYS: TIME TO SEE MUCH MORE

With more time in hand you can start to get under the skin of this fascinating city. You should also have a better chance of dry weather/wet weather options: use the dry weather option for tours on the water. It's a good idea to begin with a bus tour that will orientate you and introduce sights you may like to return to.

Take both the lake and harbour boat trips, and visit Deichstrasse and Speicherstadt. Fit the History Museum in as soon as possible to give you background information and take a bird's-eye view from one of the church towers. Ride the Maritime Circle Line to the BallinStadt Museum complex. If it is the weekend, you *must* visit St Pauli by night. Art lovers should beat a path to the Kunsthalle and see what big-name exhibitions are playing on the rest of the Art Mile.

LONGER: ENJOYING HAMBURG TO THE FULL

Once you've done everything recommended above, it's time to broaden your horizons. Hagenbeck's Zoo isn't just for kids. See where the wealthy Hamburgers live by taking the 36 bus along the Elbchaussee to Blankenese. Visit Lübeck. If you're here in summer and the weather is good, do as the Hamburgers do, hire a bike at the Hauptbahnhof and visit the Alte Land countryside on the other side of the Elbe.

◆ *The Grüner+Jahr Pressehaus (see page 45)*

Something for nothing

Hamburg is one of the wealthiest cities in Europe but you don't have to spend a fortune to enjoy it. Summer is the best season in this respect, when you can walk in the city parks, along the shore of the Elbe, and, weather permitting, even relax on the beach, all for nothing.

PARKLIFE

You can't beat a bit of semi-fresh air, and the best place to find it is in the city's largest central park, Planten un Blomen. This has beautiful botanic gardens, fountains and various activities (see page 104–5).

FREE MUSEUMS

Cultural appreciation is all the purer when unsullied by commercial transaction, and Hamburg has many opportunities for some *gratis* edification. The Museum für Völkerkunde (Ethnological Museum, see page 102) is free on Friday afternoons after 17.00, and the city university owns a couple of museums which never charge admission: the **Zoology Museum** is particularly exciting for children (🔵 Martin-Luther-King Platz 3 (off Grindelallee) ☎ (040) 42838 2276) and just across the street is the **Mineralogical Museum**, which is only open on Wednesday and Sunday afternoons. Down the road and round the corner is the **Museum for Geology & Palaeontology,** in the basement of the Geomatikum tower block, exhibiting everything from dinosaur traces to amber (🔵 Bundesstrasse 55 ☎ (040) 42838 4999). And don't forget the Museumshafen (Museum Harbour) at Övelgönne (see page 114): always open, always free!

If you want peace and quiet midweek, go a little further out to Alsterpark, on the west bank of the Aussenalster. At weekends the peace factor plummets as this becomes the city's most popular park.

WALK UNDER THE ELBE

The green-domed building next to the Landungsbrücken houses the lift to the old Elbe tunnel, which was inaugurated in 1911. Inside are four lifts, each of which descends to a depth of 24m (79ft) below the Elbe, where two tunnels lead to Steinwerder on the south side of the river. From here there is a fine view back towards the city. The tunnel is open to pedestrians and cyclists, around the clock, every day, free of charge.

AROUND THE MICHAELISKIRCHE

It's free to visit the city's most famous church, the Michaeliskirche (see page 66), although you have to pay a small charge to ascend the tower. Just next door is the exterior of the beautiful little **Karyenkamp** (again, free), with only a minimal charge to look inside. At the other end of the spectrum are the acclaimed post-modern steel-and-glass warehouse-style offices of one of Germany's largest publishers, the Grüner + Jahr Pressehaus – you can't miss them, and you wouldn't want to.

⬥ *Michaeliskirche's tower provides a great vantage point for watching passing ships*

When it rains

It rains on average one day in every three in Hamburg, so be prepared. If the weather should decide not to be too friendly, you can always hop on a sightseeing bus and take a look at Hamburg from the top of a double-decker, or pop into one of the museums. Visit a museum ship and spend a couple of hours looking at the exhibitions until the inclement weather decides to make way for the sun, then take a walk around the city centre or sit on the terrace of a café enjoying a coffee. You might even want to visit the animals at Hagenbeck's Zoo (see page 101).

The best large museums are the Museum für Hamburgische Geschichte (Hamburg History Museum, see pages 67–8), the BallinStadt Museum Complex (see pages 88–90) and the Museum für Kunst und Gewerbe (Arts and Crafts Museum, see pages 74–5). The Kunsthalle (City Art Gallery, see pages 72–4) would grace any metropolis, the temporary exhibitions at the Bucerius Art Forum next to the Rathaus (see pages 69–70) are of international calibre as are the photography exhibitions at the Deichtorhallen (see page 70). The Speicherstadt (see pages 94–5) is well worth a visit for its historical significance alone: its best general-interest attractions are Spicy's Gewürzmuseum (see page 95) and the huge Model Railway at Miniatur Wunderland (see page 92). However, there's plenty more to see here including the Hamburg Dungeon (see pages 91–2) the Speicherstadt Museum (see pages 94–5) and the Deutsches Zollmuseum (German Customs Museum, see page 90), which is free.

Other museums and galleries that might not normally be on your itinerary but which you might consider worth a detour if it really is raining non-stop are the Museum für Völkerkunde (Ethnological Museum), where the exhibits reflect Hamburg's importance as

a world shipping centre with 'souvenirs' from every continent
(see page 102), the **Altonaer (Altona) Museum** (ⓐ Museumstrasse 23
ⓘ (040) 42 81 15 14 ⓦ www.ahmburg.de/altonaer-museum) which
has a wonderful collection of figureheads from old sailing ships plus
many other maritime artefacts, the Brahms Museum (see pages 70–2)
or a tour of the Rathaus (Town Hall, see page 69).

Hamburg's shoppers are cosseted, with many of its central
shops under cover; you don't even have to get wet walking between
them, as a network of arcades and covered passageways links several
together just off Jungfernstieg. Even if you're not that keen on parting
with your money, many of the arcades are attractive buildings in
their own right and very browseable, with a particularly good range
of shops and eating establishments.

🔺 All the flavours of the world at Spicy's Gewürzmuseum in the Speicherstadt

On arrival

TIME DIFFERENCE
Hamburg follows Central European Time (CET). During Daylight Saving Time (end Mar–end Oct) the clocks are put ahead one hour.

ARRIVING
By air
Hamburg Airport lies 8 km (5 miles) north of the city centre. It is one of the largest in Germany, modern and very well equipped. Your journey into town begins with the HVV Airport Express Bus 110 from Terminal 2; change to the U1 or S1 lines at Ohlsdorf tube station. The bus leaves every ten minutes, and a single adult fare is €2.60, which includes the 20-minute onward journey to the city centre. Pay as you board the bus. Night bus 606 runs from Terminal 2 to Hauptbahnhof (Hbf, main railway station) and Rathausmarkt U-bahn station in the city centre. (As of 2009, the airport will be served by the S1 line, running every ten minutes and making the journey into town a lot more comfortable.)

Alternatively you can take Jasper's yellow Airport Express bus straight to the Hauptbahnhof. It leaves every 15–20 minutes and the journey takes 25–30 minutes. The service runs from 05.45 until midnight from the airport to Hbf, and from Hbf to the airport from 04.40 until 21.20. Adult fares are from €5 single, €8 return.

There are taxi-ranks in front of Terminal 1. A ride into the city centre should cost about €25.

Lübeck Airport (Lübeck-Blankenese) is located 8 km (5 miles) south of Lübeck, which is 59 km (37 miles) northeast of Hamburg. This is only a small airport used by some low-cost carriers, but has most facilities. A dedicated Ryanair bus runs from Hamburg ZOB (bus station over the road from Hbf) to Lübeck Airport and back, to coincide with flights. The journey takes 75–85 minutes, and costs €8 one-way. For Lübeck itself, bus 6 (at bus stop 5) runs to Lübeck Hbf via the town centre, with a journey time of 20–30 minutes. Taxis are available from outside the terminal building and are an option if you are staying in Lübeck – the journey time is around 20 minutes and costs around €18 – though it would be very expensive to hire one to Hamburg.

Hamburg Fuhlsbüttel ❶ (040) 50 75 0 Ⓦ www.ham.airport.de
Ⓝ Bus: 110 from Ohlsdorf station

Lübeck-Blankenese ❶ (0451) 58 30 10 Ⓦ www.flughafen-luebeck.de
Ⓝ Bus: 6 from Lübeck station

By rail

Trains from all over Europe run to Hamburg, terminating at the main central station **Hauptbahnhof** (Kirchenallee) or at **Altona** (Paul-Nevermann-Platz) or **Dammtor** (Theodor-Heuss-Platz). Trains approaching from the south also stop at **Harburg** (Hannoversche Strasse). All are connected to the U-bahn (underground railway) and S-bahn (overground light railway) network. ❶ infotel 01805 99 66 33 Ⓦ www.bahn.de

By water

Cruise ships dock in the main harbour, within walking distance or a short train ride of the town centre.

FINDING YOUR FEET

There's no great culture shock in Hamburg. Most people are polite, friendly and speak very good English. The pace of life is relatively relaxed, and as long as you're sensible, you should have no problems with crime (unless you're in a backstreet of St Pauli or St Georg). Watch out for the cycle path on the outer edge of the pavement – wandering onto it will result in a furious *Klingeln* of bells! And don't cross at traffic lights before the little green man comes on – you could, in theory, be fined by the police.

ORIENTATION

In the absence of a cathedral, the Rathaus (Town Hall) is the city's central landmark. This and the Binnenalster (the Inner Alster Lake) mark the *de facto* city centre. Two streets that you will probably find yourself returning to are Jungfernstieg, which runs along the front of the Binnenalster, and Mönckebergstrasse, the main shopping street, which runs from the Rathausplatz (town hall square) towards the railway station. Signposts are up all over the place for the benefit of tourists – but they are only in German, so make sure you know the name of the place to which you're headed.

The other main centre of activity is the docks, most easily reached by taking the U-bahn (U3) to Baumwall or Landungsbrücken. Both of these stations are on an elevated part of the network and offer excellent views across the port area helping you to get your bearings. The Reeperbahn, St Pauli's main street, is just a five-minute walk from here.

GETTING AROUND

The HVV (Hamburg Transport Association) runs an excellent integrated system combining rapid transit rail (U-, S- and A-Bahn trains), regional rail (R-Bahn trains), bus services and even water buses.

The U-bahn and S-bahn network makes easy work of getting around the centre and outskirts of town. As with all German underground networks, each line is designated by a colour and

IF YOU GET LOST, TRY ...

Excuse me, do you speak English?
Entschuldigen Sie, sprechen Sie Englisch?
Entshuldigen zee, shprekhen zee english?

Excuse me, is this the right way to the old town/the city centre/the tourist office/ the station/the bus station?
Entschuldigung, geht es hier zur Altstadt/zur Stadtmitte/
zur Touristeninformation/zum Bahnhof/zum Busbahnhof?
*Entshuldeegoong, gayt es here tsoor altshtat/tsoor shtatmitter/
zur Touristeninformation/tsoom baanhof/tsoom busbaanhof?*

Can you point to it on my map?
Können Sie es mir bitte auf der Karte zeigen?
Kernen see es meer bitter owf der kaarte tsygen?

number. Clear signposting, indicator boards on the platform and
on-board announcements make sure you know in which direction
you are moving and what the next stop is. The same is true for the
bus service, which fills in the gaps left by the rail services and is
most useful for short hops, e.g. along the main shopping streets,
or when you want to see a bit of the scenery, such as on Bus 36 to
Blankenese (see pages 124–9).

Tickets

Tickets for the U-bahn, S-bahn and all regional trains must be purchased
in advance. The system relies on an honesty basis with no ticket

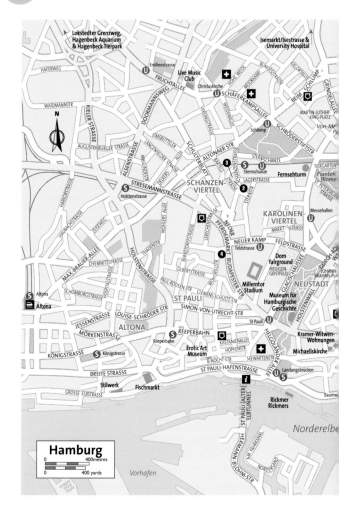

Hamburg

0   400 metres
0   400 yards

Lokstedter Grenzweg,
Hagenbeck Aquarium
& Hagenbeck Tierpark

Isemarkt/Isestrasse &
University Hospital

Live Music Club

FRUCHTALLEE

HAFERWEG

WAIDMANNSTR

Christuskirche

SCHÄFERKAMPSALLEE

DOORMANNSWEG

KIELER STRASSE

MARTIN-LUTHER-
KING-PLATZ

Von-Me

Schlump

SCHRÖDERSTIFTSTR

AUGUSTENBURGER STRASSE

EIMSBÜTTELER

LANGENFELDER STRASSE

SCHULTERBLATT

ALTONAER STR

ALSENSTRASSE

WEIDENSTIEG

STRASSE

STERNSCHANZE

TIERGARTEN

Planten u.
Blome

Sternschanze

Fernsehturm

SCHANZEN-
VIERTEL

LAGERSTRASSE

STRESEMANNSTRASSE

Holstenstrasse

KAROLINEN-
VIERTEL

MARKT- STRASSE

Messehallen

HOLSTENSTRASSE

NEUER PFERDEMARKT

NEUER KAMP

FELDSTRASSE

Feldstrasse

MAX-BRAUER-ALLEE

CHEMNITZSTRASSE

GILBERTSTRASSE

BUDAPESTER STR

Dom fairground

HEILIGEN-
GEISTFELD

GLACISCHAUSSEE

SCHOMBURGSTRASSE

PAUL-ROOSEN-STR

CLEMENS-SCHULTZ-STR

JOHANN BRAHMS-PL

Altona

LOUISE-SCHRÖDER STR

JESSENSTRASSE

SIMON-VON-UTRECHT-STR

ST PAULI

Millerntor Stadium

Museum für
Hamburgische
Geschichte

NEUSTADT

HOLSTENWALL

Altona

St Pauli

MÖRKENSTRASSE

ALTONA

REEPERBAHN

Reeperbahn

Kramer-Witwen-
Wohnungen

Michaeliskirche

KÖNIGSTRASSE

Königstrasse

Erotic Art
Museum

HOPFENSTR

HELGOLÄNDER

B-NOCHT-STR

SEEWARTENSTR

Landungsbrücken

BREITE STRASSE

ST PAULI-HAFENSTRASSE

Stilwerk

Fischmarkt

GROSSE ELBSTRASSE

Rickmer Rickmers

Baumw

Norderelbe

ST PAULI (ALTER)
ELBTUNNEL

HERMANN-BLOHM-STR

Vorhafen

NORD

M.M. RÄHDAHL

Hamburg
Rotherbaum Tennis Centre
Hallerstrasse
Planetarium, Stadtpark & Hindenburgstrasse
Alsterpark
Mundsburg
English Theatre
Museum für Völkerkunde
AVERHOFFSTRASSE
HERBERT-WEICHMANN-STRASSE
HORVIG
SCHÖNE AUSSICHT
PAPENHUDER STRASSE
MUNDSBURGER DAMM
EILENAU
ROTHENBAUM
Aussenalster
HOHENFELDE
Uhlandstrasse
GRAUMANNSWEG
IFFLANDSTRASSE
SECHSLINGSPFORTE
BARCASTRASSE
Alsterschwimmhalle
Lübecker Strasse
Dammtor
Dammtor
AN DER ALSTER
KOPPEL
LANGE REIHE
ROSTOCKER STRASSE
BERLINER TOR
Lochmühlenstrasse
Stephansplatz
KENNEDYBRÜCKE
ESPLANADE LOMBARDSBRÜCKE
STEINDAMM
ST GEORG
Berliner Tor
Opera House
Gänsemarktpassage
Kunsthalle
Gänsemarkt
Binnenalster
Hauptbahnhof Nord
NORDSTRASSE
Hauptbahnhof
Hauptbahnhof Süd
ADENAUERALLEE
Hanseviertel
Jungfernstieg
Europa Passage
Levantehaus
ZOB
K. SCHUMACHERALLEE
NORDERSTRASSE
HAMMERBROOK
Bleichenhof
Museum für Kunst und Gewerbe
SPALDINGSTRASSE
NORDKANALSTRASSE
Rathaus
Rathaus
Jacobikirche
Mönckebergstr
STEINSTR
MÖNCKEBERGSTR
Steinstrasse
Kunsthaus
Hammerbrook
NAGELSWEG
Hopfenmarkt
Stadthausbrücke
Freie Akademie der Künste
Messberg
Rödingsmarkt
WILLY-BRANDT-STRASSE
ALTSTADT
HÖGERDAMM
AMSINCKSTRASSE
WENDENSTR
DOMSTR
KATHARINENSTR
Speicherstadt Museum
BANKSTRASSE
Miniatur Wunderland
Hamburg Dungeon
KLOSTERTOR
Spicy's Gewürzmuseum
AM SANDTORKAI
BROOKTOR
MAGDEBURGER STR
Oberhafen
AM KAISERKAI
DÜSSERKAI
TEERHOF
VERSMANNSTRASSE
Baakenhafen

POI
U-Bahn
S-Bahn
Information
Police Station
Airport
Railway Stn
Bus Station
Hospital

THE HAMBURG CARD

The Hamburg Card gives unlimited first-class travel on all public transport in the Greater Hamburg area and also grants you free or reduced-price admission to many attractions and excursions, including the Rathaus, St Michael's Church and sightseeing trips around the city, the port, on the River Alster and the lakes.

A one-day card costs €8, a three-day is €18 and is valid for one adult and three children up to the age of 14 years. You *must* sign and date it before use, otherwise it will not be valid. The Hamburg Card can be purchased at any Hamburg tourist office (see page 152).

barriers and few inspectors. However if you are caught without a ticket you will be fined heavily. Make sure you are carrying small change for the ticket machine (see prices below), and leave enough time before catching your train to have the ridiculously complicated ticket machine explained to you! You can also purchase tickets from the driver when boarding your bus. You can buy individual tickets per journey, starting at €1.30 and increasing as you pass through more zones, but if you are around for a day or more it is worth investing in one of the passes listed opposite. Group tickets and family tickets are also available (under 6s do not need a ticket and travel free of charge on the HVV network). Further information ☎ (040) 300 51 300 Ⓦ www.hvv.de

All-day ticket The central area starts at €6, valid for unlimited travel by one adult and three children aged 6 to 14 from the time of purchase on the date of issue until expiry at 06.00 on the following day. The **9AM Day Card** offers the same but is only valid after 09.00; cost is €5.10. These tickets are valid on the Underground, S-bahn, buses and water buses.

Three-day ticket Valid for unlimited travel by one person throughout the Greater Hamburg Area, €15. This ticket is transferable.

Taxis

Taxis may be hailed on the street when the sign on the roof is illuminated. Journeys within the city are metered, journeys outside are negotiable. Rates are comparable to other northern European cities.

CAR HIRE

Driving into Hamburg has all the drawbacks of driving and parking as in any other major city and is not recommended. If you are hiring a car consult the airport website (Ⓦ www.ham.airport.de or Ⓦ www.flughaten-luebeck.de) for directions. Note that you can leave your car free of charge at one of the HVV park-and-ride facilities (see Ⓦ www.hvv.de for more information) at rapid transit

🔺 Public transport on the water, Hamburg style

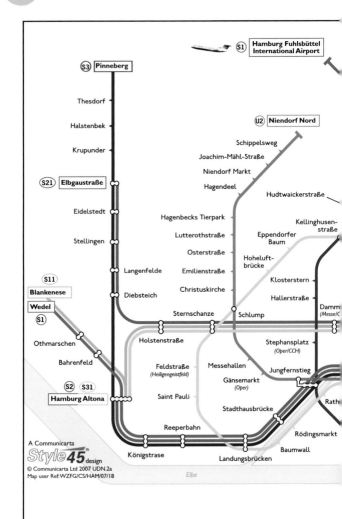

S1 Hamburg Fuhlsbüttel International Airport

S3 Pinneberg

Thesdorf

Halstenbek

Krupunder

U2 Niendorf Nord

Schippelsweg

Joachim-Mähl-Straße

Niendorf Markt

Hagendeel

Hudtwaickerstraße

S21 Elbgaustraße

Eidelstedt

Stellingen

Hagenbecks Tierpark

Lutterothstraße

Osterstraße

Emilienstraße

Christuskirche

Kellinghusen-straße

Eppendorfer Baum

Hoheluft-brücke

Klosterstern

Hallerstraße

Langenfelde

Diebsteich

S11

Blankenese

Wedel

S1

Sternschanze

Schlump

Damm (Messe/C

Othmarschen

Bahrenfeld

Holstenstraße

Stephansplatz (Oper/CCH)

S2 S31

Hamburg Altona

Feldstraße (Heiligengeistfeld)

Messehallen

Gänsemarkt (Oper)

Jungfernstieg

Saint Pauli

Stadthausbrücke

Rath

Reeperbahn

Königstrasse

Landungsbrücken

Rödingsmarkt

Baumwall

A Communicarta
Style 45 design
© Communicarta Ltd 2007 UDN.2a
Map user Ref: WZFG/CS/HAM/07/18

Elbe

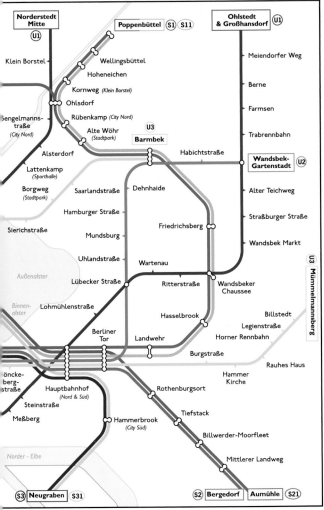

and regional rail stations, which avoids the hassle of inner-city driving and parking.

Car hire operators at Hamburg airport include:

Avis ① (040) 50 75 23 14 Ⓦ www.avis.com

Budget ① (040) 50 75 38 11 Ⓦ www.budget.com

Europcar ① (040) 50 02 17 0 Ⓦ www.europcar.com

Hertz ① (040) 59 35 13 67 Ⓦ www.hertz.com

National Car Rental/ Alamo ① (040) 50 75 23 01
Ⓦ www.nationalcar.com or www.alamo.com

Sixt Affiliated to German Wings, whose passengers should book through the German Wings website to obtain a discount.
① (01805) 26 25 25 Ⓦ www.e-sixt.com

● *The view from the Michaeliskirche offers great panoramas of the city*

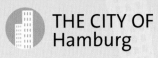

THE CITY

The city centre

Most of Hamburg's historical centre was burned down in two
dreadful conflagrations, the great fire of 1842 which destroyed a
quarter of the city centre, then in July 1943 it suffered unimaginable
horror when it became the first city in the world to suffer a firestorm,
at the hands of Allied bombing (see page 64). Consequently what
you will see today is mostly modern with only a few surviving
churches and historic houses spared the flames and other ravages
of time. It's not unattractive, however, with some striking modern
buildings cheek by jowl with neoclassical façades (some new, some
re-created, some restored) and a good sense of space.

Virtually nothing remains of the old city walls but the lines are
still clearly marked on the map by the ring road that encircles the
city centre. Holstenwall and Gorch-Fock Wall form the western
boundary, running into the Lombardsbrücke, which divides the
Binnenalster (inner lake) from the Aussenalster (outer lake). It is
from here that the classic picture-postcard photographs of the
city are taken. Glockengiesserwall swings south-east past the
main railway station (Hauptbahnhof) becoming Steintorwall
and Klosterwall. At Deichtorplatz, just before Klosterwall reaches
the docks, Willy-Brandt-Strasse slices at right angles across it,
providing a neat north–south dividing line. The city centre
covered in this chapter is the area to the north of here.

SIGHTS & ATTRACTIONS

Aussenalster and Binnenalster (Alster Lake)
Most major European cities have a special square or piazza;
Hamburg – like Geneva – has a lake, divided into two distinct parts.

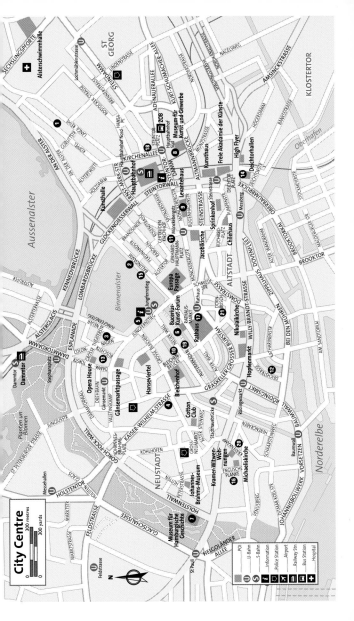

HERR HUMMEL

Wherever you go in the city centre you will come across the same curious statue again and again, of a clown-like figure with a yoke across his shoulders carrying two buckets of water. The statues are always the same, though each is painted and decorated individually by their various sponsors. Count them as you go; there are 100 in total. They commemorate 'Hans Hummel', real name Johann Wilhelm Bentz, born in 1787 at Grosse Drehbahn 36. Hummel was a mean and miserly water-carrier teased by the city children and given the derisive nickname 'Hummel, Hummel' (meaning bumble bee). Because of the load he was carrying he couldn't catch the children but simply shouted 'Mors, Mors!' which in Low German means 'Arses, arses!'. For some reason this captured the Hamburg public imagination (in much the same way as televison catchphrases do now) and if you shout 'Hummel, Hummel!' in the street even today, over 200 years after Bentz died, the reaction will be predictably coarse!

While the smaller Binnenalster provides a neat blue concrete-flanked welcome mat to the city, the bucolic Aussenalster is its pride and joy, home to millionaires and consulates. Hamburgers flock here year round; on sunny summer days to take to the water and laze in the parks, and in winter, ice thickness permitting, to skate. It takes approximately three hours if you want to walk all the way around.

▶ *Hummelmänner prepare to take the city by storm!*

There are three main boat tours. The short lake tour, the Alster
Rundfahrt, takes just under one hour, roughly following the lake
perimeter; the longer Alster-Kreuz-Fahrt harks back to the days
when steamers were an important part of the public transport
network and it tacks across the lake, making nine stops on a
leisurely two-hour cruise. You can make it last much longer by
hopping on and hopping off, visiting the fashionable cafés and
restaurants. A third variation is the Kanal Fahrt, which adds the
canals around the docks to a lake tour, specifically those canals
interwining the Speicherstadt. Keep an eye out for the zero-
emission ships being integrated into the fleet.

THE DEAD CITY

'History's first mass fire began on the night of July 27, 1943, in
Hamburg – created by Allied incendiary raids. Within 20 minutes,
two-thirds of the buildings within an area of 4.5 square miles
were on fire. It took fewer than six hours for the fire to completely
burn an area of more than five square miles. Damage analysts
called it the "Dead City". Wind speeds were of hurricane force;
air temperatures were 204–260°C (400–500°F). Between
60,000 and 100,000 people were killed in the attack.' (From
an article on 'Firestorm Physics' in the *Bulletin of the Atomic
Scientists 2005*). According to the church's own figures, around
34,000 people perished between 25 July and 3 August 1943
during the Allied Air Forces' Operation Gomorrha, and in total
55,000 Hamburg civilians were killed during the whole of
World War II.

HighFlyer

Hamburg's highest vantage point: a hot-air balloon anchored by
a steel cable, which rises to a height of 150 m (492 ft). The balloon
is stationed right next-door to the Deichtorhallen and a balloon
ticket allows you a hefty discount on the Deichtorhalle admission
fee. Each trip on the balloon lasts approximately 15 minutes and
the views are spectacular. The balloon pilots recommend going
up at twilight and watching the lights go on all over town.
ⓐ Deichtorstrasse 1–2 ❶ weather hotline (040) 30 08 69 69, group
reservations (040) 30 08 69 72 Ⓦ www.highflyer-hamburg.de
🕙 10.00–22.00 Ⓝ U-bahn: U1 to Steinstrasse .

Jacobikirche (St James' Church)

This large Gothic hall-style church dates from the mid-14th century
and was destroyed by bombing in 1944. Reconstructed in 1962, it has
several points of interest that make it worth a visit. On the north
wall are two excellent examples of Northern German painting:
David Kindt's *The Rich Man and Death* (1662) warns against wealth
resulting in pride, while Joachim Luhn's fine panorama depicts
Hamburg as it looked in the late 17th century. Note the church's
three carved and painted altar table screens, its fine alabaster
and marble pulpit (1610) and its celebrated 1693 organ by master
craftsman Arp Schnitger. You can hear it booming out every Thursday
at noon. There are also regular concerts here July–early September on
Tuesdays at 20.00. Tours of the church are given in English if requested
on the first Thursday of the month at 16.00. If your German is up to
it ask if you can use the lift to the top of the tower (not generally open
to the public) to enjoy the views. ⓐ Steinstrasse ❶ (040) 30 37 370
Ⓦ www.jacobus.de 🕙 07.00–18.00 Ⓝ U-bahn: U3 to Mönckebergstrasse

Kramer-Witwen-Wohnungen (Almshouses for Merchants' Widows)

Next door to St Michaeliskirche is a picturesque block of tiny
almshouses, hidden away behind a gated courtyard, which
were built in the 1670s for merchants' widows. Number 10 is
open as a small museum while a restaurant (see pages 85–6)
occupies a number of other houses. The rest have been
turned into souvenir shops and galleries. ❸ Krayenkamp 10
❶ (040) 37 50 19 88 ❹ 10.00–17.00 Tues–Sun, closed Mon
Ⓝ S-bahn: S1, S3 to Stadthausbrücke; U-bahn: U3 to Baumwall or
Rödingsmarkt; Bus: 37 to Michaeliskirche. Small admission charge

Michaeliskirche (St Michaelis' Church)

'Michel' is a symbol of the city and has always been a landmark to
homecoming sailors. The tower, 82 m (269 ft) high, has a distinctive
copper covering and its clock face, measuring 8 m (26 ft) in diameter
(larger than London's Big Ben), is the biggest in Germany. The current
church dates from 1906–12, built in the style of the mid-18th century
and rebuilt after World War II. Its round-tiered baroque-style interior
is very much like a concert hall, a function it fulfils regularly, and it
is certainly worth being here at 12.00 (daily) when all three of its
organs are played. The views from its tower over the port and city
are superb. In the lower part of the tower there is an audio-visual
show on the history of Hamburg (in German only) and there is an
exhibition in the crypt on the history of the church. ❸ Englische
Planke ❶ (040) 37 67 81 00 ❿ www.st-michaelis.de ❹ 09.00–17.30
Mon–Sat, 10.30–17.30 Sun, May–Oct; 10.00–16.30 Mon–Sat, 10.30–16.30
Sun, Nov–Apr Ⓝ S-bahn: S1, S3 to Stadthausbrücke; U-bahn: U3 to
Baumwall or Rödingsmarkt; Bus: 37 to Michaeliskirche. Separate
admission charges to tower, crypt and audio-visual show

⬤ *'Michel' stands by the harbour, surrounded by modern Hamburg*

Museum für Hamburgische Geschichte (Hamburg History Museum)

This is easily Hamburg's finest museum, covering just about every aspect of the city in a lively captivating manner with many large-scale exhibits and captions for all displays and objects in perfect English. Pick up a floor plan to help you navigate around its three, often confusing, floors. On the ground floor the huge model of the Temple of Solomon is very impressive. Don't miss Hamburg in the 20th century, a lively exhibition with domestic and shop reconstructions together with music and videos. On the first floor, there is a full-size reconstruction of part of a cog (a traditional sailing ship) and a similar reconstruction of the bridge of the Dampfer (Steamship) *Werner*, where you can step aboard and view how Hamburg harbour appeared in 1938. *Medieval Hamburg* tells how pirates terrorised the port and shows pirate skulls pierced by huge nails which were then affixed to public places as a warning. The second floor features the history of the Jews in Hamburg, rooms from Deichstrasse (see page 94) and the largest model railway in Europe (on a scale 1:32). Check out the superb website before you visit and do go to the museum's excellent Café Fees (see page 80). ⓐ Holstenwall 24 ⓣ (040) 42 81 32 ⓦ www.hamburgmuseum.de ⓛ 10.00–17.00 Tues–Sat, 10.00–18.00 Sun, closed Mon; model railway open for 25 minutes only, on each hour, 11.00, 12.00, 14,00, 15.00 Tues–Sat; 11.00, 12.00, 14.00, 15.00, 16.00 Sun ⓝ U-bahn:U3 to St Pauli

Nikolaikirche (St Nicholas' Church)

Before the *Hamburger Feuersturm* of 1943 (see page 64) this was the fourth-highest church in the world, reaching a height of 147.3 m (483 ft). Today it remains a deliberately unreconstructed soot-blackened ruin – a memorial to the victims of war and violence, *gegen das Vergessen* (lest we forget). The exception is the steeple, ironically used during that fateful night as a target point by Allied bombers. Ironic too, that it was designed by the renowned British architect George Gilbert Scott in 1874. It has been equipped with a lift that offers one of Hamburg's finest viewpoints. A small glass pyramid marks the entrance to the former undercroft, now used as an exhibition area with a video on the destruction (commentary in German only) and a harrowing exhibition of photographs showing the damage to buildings and people. A commentary sheet available in English, explains the Allies' political theory of 'Morale Bombing' and how it was decided that the main goal aimed at would be civilian morale 'in particular that of the workers in the defence industries'. It explains how Hamburg was targeted in retaliation for the bombing of Coventry and Birmingham, yet despite the dreadful scale of retribution maintains a dignified and remarkable equanimity. ❸ Willy-Brandt-Strasse 60 ❶ (040) 37 11 25 Ⓦ www.mahnmal-st-nikolai.de ❹ 10.30–18.30 (tower and visitor centre) Ⓝ U-bahn: U3 to Rödingsmarkt

Rathaus (Town Hall)

This splendid castle-like edifice, adorned with statues and spiky pinnacles, is much younger than it looks, having been built in 1887. They proudly claim it has 647 rooms ('more than Buckingham Palace') but if you want to see more than the vestibule (note the macabre clock above the main entrance door, with death on the coffin which strikes the hour) you'll need to join a tour. English-language tours run every hour at 15 minutes past the hour; however, a minimum number of English-speaking people buying tickets for that tour is required or you will be moved onto the next (German-speaking) tour. Highlights among the many opulent rooms are the Debating Chamber, where the 121 members of the city-state's parliament sit, and the magnificent Great Banquet Hall, where each chandelier has 278 lights. ❸ Rathausplatz ❶ (040) 428 31 20 10 ❹ Open 10.00–15.15 (last tour) Mon–Thur, 10.00–13.15 (last tour) Fri–Sun Ⓝ U-bahn : U3 to Rathaus Charge for tour

CULTURE

Bucerius-Kunst-Forum (Bucerius Art Forum)

Adjacent to the Rathaus and occupying a handsome classical building, this gallery stages four major temporary exhibitions a year, ranging from the art of the ancient world to classic modern art. Like many of its fellow art establishments, it has a fine café. 🅐 Rathausmarkt 2 🅣 (040) 36 09 960 🅦 www.buceriuskunstforum.de 🅛 11.00–19.00 🅝 U-bahn: U3 to Rathaus. Admission charge

Deichtorhallen

The impressive iron-and-glass halls of the old wholesale flower market, built 1911–14, are now devoted to photography. There is a permanent collection, the Sammlung F C Gundlach, which comprises works from the fields of documentary and fashion photography as well as photographic works by fine artists and temporary exhibitions of international standing. 🅐 Deichtorstrasse 1–2 🅣 (040) 32 10 30 🅦 www.deichtorhallen.de 🅛 10.00–18.00 Tues–Sun, closed Mon 🅝 U-bahn: U1 to Steinstrasse. Admission charge

Johannes-Brahms-Museum

Johannes Brahms was born in Hamburg in 1833 in Speckstrasse. Unfortunately the house was destroyed in 1943, so the society dedicated to the great composer decided to create a museum in neighbouring Peterstrasse, itself destroyed in 1943 but convincingly re-created to its original baroque appearance and now one of the city's loveliest streets. Among the mementos here are Brahms' letters and photographs, signatures, concert programmes, scores and sheet music. Larger exhibits include the composer's writing desk and one of his pianos. In fact Brahms spent relatively little of his adult life in his native city. He settled in Vienna in 1868 and died there in 1897. 🅐 Peterstrasse 39 🅣 (040) 45 21 58 🅦 www.brahms-hamburg.de 🅛 10.00–13.00 Tues & Thur;

🅓 *The almshouses for merchants' widows belong to another era*

11.00–14.00 first and third Sun in month, Jun–Sept ⊙ U-bahn: U3 to St Pauli. Admission charge

Kontorhäuser

Hamburg's *Kontorhäuser* office blocks are colossal, sombre, red-brick buildings clustered around the Burchardplatz. The most famous is the ship-like Chilehaus, built in 1922 in Expressionist style, taking its name from the country where its owner, Henry B Sloman, made his fortune by shipping saltpetre to Hamburg. Its neighbour the Sprinkenhof is another huge office complex, which cars can drive right into.

Kunsthalle (City Art Gallery)

Hamburg's Kunsthalle is one of the finest and largest German galleries outside Berlin. It comprises three interconnected buildings and the emphasis is on German and north European works. If you have the stamina you can follow it chronologically from North German art in the 1400s all the way through to the 21st-century installation in the Galerie der Gegenwart (Gallery of Contemporary Art), housed in its own striking white modernist cube building. Beware, though, that the layout is not particularly easy to follow, even with the map leaflet *Was ist wo* ('What is where').

If you intend to view the collection chronologically start your tour at the classical main entrance, nearest the Hauptbahnhof. Among the Alte Meister (Old Masters) highlights are the works of Master Bertram of Minden (Germany's first accomplished master painter known by name), Lucas Cranach, Rembrandt, Claude Lorrain and Peter Paul Rubens. German artists come to the fore in the *19. Jahrhundert* (19th century) section, with some striking works by Caspar David Friedrichs and Phillip Otto Runge. Also in this section are instantly recognisable French impressionist works by Manet, Monet, Renoir and co. A small 20th-century section includes works by Kokoschka and Klee.

It's a good idea to take a break in the lovely Café Liebermann, something of an artwork in itself. At this point you can either take the stairs to the Hubertus-Wald-Forum, which is devoted to temporary exhibitions excluding contemporary art, or head to the Gallery of Contemporary Art, whose remit begins in the 1960s, and also begins on the bottom floor with its main temporary exhibitions. These often feature artists of a high international reputation.

There are a further four floors of contemporary art, including a large collection of American Pop Art (Andy Warhol, Robert Rauschenberg et al) alongside works by the most famous German contemporary artist, Joseph Beuys. The rest of the gallery space is devoted to temporary exhibitions, which invariably include multi-

THE ART MILE

The stretch of road that runs between the Deichtorhallen and the Kunsthalle is known as the Kunstmeile, or Art Mile (see pages 18–19). In addition to these two major establishments is the Museum für Kunst und Gewerbe (Arts and Crafts Museum, see page 74), set just back off the main road, and almost opposite the Deichtorhallen are three lesser known avant-garde art venues; the **Freie Akademie der Künste** (Ⓦ www.akademie-der-kuenste.de), the **Kunstverein in Hamburg** (Ⓦ www.kunstverein.de) and the **Kunsthaus** (Ⓦ www.kunsthaushamburg.de). All stage contemporary art exhibitions; see their respective websites for more details.

media installations. This gallery also has a good café.
Ⓐ Glockengiesserwall Ⓣ (040) 428 131 200 Ⓦ www.hamburger-kunsthalle.de Ⓛ 10.00–18.00 Tues–Sun, 10.00–21.00 Thur, closed Mon Ⓢ all lines to Hauptbahnhof. Admission charge; reduced price for 'The Blue Hour' the last hour before museum closing time (does not include Hubertus-Wald-Forum)

Museum für Kunst und Gewerbe (Arts and Crafts Museum)
Housed in dozens of small rooms over four floors, this old-fashioned jackdaw's nest varies from the Art of the Ancient World to temporary exhibits on contemporary subjects. Pick up a floor plan in English and be sure to see the Musical Instruments and the Art Nouveau rooms.

Start on the ground floor with medieval art, represented by bronzes, goldsmiths' work and ivory objects of exquisite quality. The Renaissance collections include some world-class bronze works and tapestries, outstanding inlaid cabinets, furniture and artistically made cupboards as well as beautiful scientific instruments from the Renaissance and baroque periods. Complete period rooms from Hamburg houses of the 17th–19th centuries are a highlight of this floor. Begin the first floor with the Historical Keyboards collection, which began in 1890 with an endowment of 10,000 Marks to the museum by Hans von Bülow, a friend of Johannes Brahms (see pages 70–2). Today the museum possesses some 400 European exhibits, many made in Hamburg workshops, and about 30 instruments from other parts of the world. Some of these are demonstrated on the first Sunday of the month at 16.00.

The Ancient World collection shows works of art from the Ancient Orient, Egypt and Classical Antiquity. In a Japanese tea-house the tea ceremony is normally performed on each third weekend in the month. Each visitor is served a bowl of green tea and a Japanese sweet at the end of the ceremony, which lasts about an hour (small additional charge). Don't miss the café-restaurant Destille, also on this floor (see page 82, €2 fee for entry to café only).

The Art Nouveau/Jugendstil section goes back to the museum's founder, Justus Brinckmann, who took advantage of the World Exhibition in Paris in 1900 to purchase and develop a large collection of contemporary applied art centred on furniture and room decors (there are a number of intact interiors), wall hangings, textiles, lamps, decorative objects in glass, metal, ceramics and sculptures plus books and jewellery.

The second floor is devoted mostly to design and photography with regular special exhibitions. **③** Steintorplatz **①** (040) 428 54 27 32 **⑩** www.mkg-hamburg.de **🕒** 10.00–18.00 Tues–Sun, 10.00–21.00 Thur, closed Mon **Ⓝ** all lines to Hauptbahnhof. Admission charge

RETAIL THERAPY

The city centre is the focus for Hamburg's love affair with shopping. The main retail street is Mönckebergstrasse, but, in the event that you can't find what you want along here, there are ten major indoor centres with varying degrees of exclusivity. The emphasis throughout is on conspicuous consumption of national and international brand names in fashion, jewellery and high-class furnishings; there are few bargains or individualistic shops here.

Mönckebergstrasse
Both the Mönckebergstrasse and its parallel, the pedestrianised Spitalerstrasse, are home to the high-street chains. If you're looking for clothing or shoes, there's plenty of choice, but it's none too

different from what you've got back home. For more interesting contents you need to veer off the main thoroughfare.

The markets on the Gerhart-Hauptmann-Platz provide an amusing distraction, and there are a few gems in the side-streets: Michelle Records at Gertrudenkirchhof for serious vinyl fans, or Dr Götze Land & Karte at Alstertor (behind the Thalia Theatre) for a monumental selection of travel books and maps. The most exciting shop on the Mönckebergstrasse is Karstadt Sporthaus, dedicated to sports equipment and games, and Europe's biggest sports goods retailer. You can try out golf clubs and tennis rackets actually hitting balls into simulators, a wind tunnel to find out how breathable your new outdoor jacket is and an artificial mountain environment to test your new footwear. There's also a rooftop area, enclosed by a safety net, devoted to an ice skating rink in winter and a multi-purpose sports field in summer, complete with a four-lane 100 m (109 yds) tartan track, where you can try out more goods before purchasing.

There are several malls off Mönckebergstrasse. Drop into Levantehaus, which relies more on the quality of shops and refreshment outlets than international brand names, or stroll through the Europa Passage (see page 22) to the Binnenalster Lake.

On and around Jungfernstieg

The grand old lady of retail is the **Alsterhaus**, the city's oldest department store and something of an icon. It boasts a huge cosmetics department, Hamburg's biggest wine choice and a splendid fine-foods department. Its neighbours on the Jungfernstieg include high-class jewellers and fashion designers such as **Rene Lezard**.

▶ *Mönckebergstrasse is a pedestrianised paradise for shoppers*

MACCA'S FAB GEAR

Although Karstadt would no longer be the first shopping choice for hip young musicians, it was here that the Beatles bought some of their clothes when in Hamburg in the 1960s. 'You could get great leather gear in Hamburg', Paul McCartney told the newspapers. 'We went home to Liverpool wearing the clothes we had bought in Hamburg. Everyone thought we were the latest "in" group from Germany and remarked on how well we spoke English!'

Neuer Wall runs off here, a street devoted to affluent designer label collectors including **Jil Sander**. In a typical Hanseatic red-brick building with soaring domes, is the **Hanseviertel** mall on Grosse Bleichen. On the opposite side of Grosse Bleichen is the Kaufmannshaus, a mall in a steel-and-glass building that is worth seeing, as is the **Bleichenhof** mall. On the lake side of Jungfernstieg, a few doors down from the Alsterpavillon, is the **Nivea Beauty Centre**, where you can book yourself in for a massage or a makeover. Between Nivea and Hotel Vier Jahreszeiten the pedestrianised Colonnaden (named after the covered arcades that dominate the street, and host to weekend antique fayres) offers a few interesting shops: **Pfeifen Tesch** for cigar connoisseurs and pipe smokers, **Chocolat du Monde** for the sweet of tooth, **der Bocksbeutel** for high–quality German wines and **zweitausendeins** for low-price CDs. Again, plenty of cafés and bistros to choose from for a break, or turn off into the **Gänsemarktpassage**.

TAKING A BREAK

Although Hamburg may not have the same reputation for its café culture as, say, Italian cities or Vienna, a coffee and cake in the centre of town is invariably a treat. This is due in no small part to the large number of shops, the well-heeled clientele and the city's heritage and expertise in shipping tea and coffee. Competition means prices are usually reasonable too.

Café Koppel £ ❶ In the artisans' house near the bottom of Lange Reihe, just round the corner from Hauptbahnhof. Menu 100% vegetarian, including all-day breakfast and lunchtime specials. Homebaked cakes and homemade jams belong to the café's repertoire. Courtyard garden. ➒ Koppel 66 ➊ (040) 24 92 33 Ⓦ www.koppel66.de Ⓛ 10.00–23.00 Ⓝ all lines to Hauptbahnhof

Café Wien £ ❷ Actually on the water with a wonderful view of the comings and goings on Jungfernstieg. Lunchtime special from €5.70, afternoon coffee and cake. This café boat is popular with city workers for early-evening drinks. ➒ Ballindamm ➊ (040) 33 63 42 Ⓛ 11.00–24.00 Mon–Thur, 11.00–01.00 Fri, 10.00–01.00 Sat, 10.00–23.00 Sun Ⓝ all lines to Jungfernstieg

Der Bocksbeutel in den Colonnaden £ ❸ Wine bar on the Colonnaden pedestrian precinct behind the Opera House. Admire the covered arcades after which the street is named while sampling German wines or traditional schnapps made from fruit. Snacks available. ➒ Colonnaden 54 ➊ (040) 345 102 ➊ (040) 463 304 Ⓦ www.derbocksbeutel.de Ⓛ 10.30–20.00 (last orders) Mon–Sat, 15.00–19.00 Sun Ⓝ U-bahn: U2 to Gänsemarkt

Edelcurry £ ❹ Hamburg's favourite meal and culinary claim to fame: Currywurst und Pommes, otherwise known as sausage & chips. Variations on a theme offered here, in an elegant restaurant situation, with a selection of exotic sauces to choose from. ⓐ Grosse Bleichen 68 ❶ (040) 357 16 262 ⓦ www.edelcurry.de ❶11.00–22.00 Mon–Sat, 12.00–20.00 Sun ⓝ S-bahn: S1, S3 to Stadthausbrücke

Alex im Alsterpavilion ££ ❺ Highly popular on a summer's day, owing largely to its location opposite the Alsterhaus store and next to the Jungfernstieg boat stage. The quality is acceptable, though you may have to wait to be served. ⓐ Jungfernstieg 54 ❶ (040) 350 18 70 ⓦ www.alexgastro.de ❶ 09.00/10.00–late (summer 01.00)

Arkaden-Café ££ ❻ On a summer's day when the geranium-decked riverside terrace is open, this is the place to be in the centre of town, crammed with out-of-town visitors, shoppers and ladies who lunch. Get there early to get a good seat. ⓐ Alsterarkaden 910 ❶ (040) 35 76 06 30 ❶ 09.00–late

Café Fees ££ ❼ This splendid Orangery-style building mixes Gothic fittings, ornate chandeliers, art nouveau and 21st-century style perfectly. It has a beautiful glass-covered courtyard with patio heaters for all year use. There is a short but interesting full menu of modern German dishes and this is a popular meeting place for Sunday brunch. ⓐ Holstenwall 24 (Museum of Hamburg History) ❶ (040) 35 31 32 ⓦ www.fees-hamburg.de ❶ 10.00–02.00 Tues–Sun, 10.00–04.00 Fri–Sat, closed Mon Meals served 10.00–15.00 Tues–Sat, Thur–Sat 18.00–24.00 ⓝ U-bahn: U3 to St Pauli

● *Hamburg relaxes in the cafés of the Alsterarkaden*

Destille ££ ❽ It is worth a trip to the Arts and Crafts museum for the café alone, decorated in the style of a *Gaststube* (traditional tea parlour) around the turn of the 20th century, albeit with valuable paintings around the walls. The cold buffet of Scandinavian and German meats and dishes is excellent. See page 75 for details. Entrance to café only, small charge, closed Mon

Die Rösterei ££ ❾ Lively modern café useful for a shopping break at the top end of the Mönckebergstrasse. Both upstairs in Levantehaus and pavement café, weather permitting. ⓐ Levantehaus, Mönckebergstrasse 7 ❶ (040) 30 39 37 35 ❶ 09.00–21.00, closed Sun (winter)

Grill & Green ££ ❿ Light, airy, modern bistro-style restaurant with a terrace on the Alster canal in the basement of the Bleichenhof shopping arcade. The food is up-to-date, healthy, fresh and good value; salads, pastas, grills, wok dishes, tortillas and so on. ⓐ Bleichenbrücke 9 ❶ (040) 35 30 50 ⓦ www.grillandgreen.de ❶ 12.00–23.00 Mon–Sat, 10.30–23.00 Sun ⓝ S-bahn: S1, S3 to Stadthausbrücke

Le Paquebot ££ ⓫ Set just off Mönckebergstrasse, the art deco style cafè-restaurant of the Thalia Theatre is an excellent spot for a light

CAFÉS WITH A VIEW
The café of the Alsterhaus looks directly onto the Binnenalster from its fourth-floor location; Flow Restaurant bistro at Karstadt Sport has a fifth-floor roof garden with views over the centre of town.

lunch or a coffee while shopping. ⓐ Gerhart-Hauptmann-Platz
❶ (040 32 65 19 ❷ 11.00–01.00 Mon–Sat, closed Sun ❸ U-bahn:
U3 to Mönckebergstrasse

AFTER DARK

Most of Hamburg's nightlife takes place in the St Pauli area and
elsewhere, but the city centre still offers a good choice of bars,
restaurants and entertainment options.

RESTAURANTS

Alt-Hamburger Aalspeicher ££ ⓬ Beautiful traditional restaurant in
one of Deichstrasse's 17th-century houses, specialising in traditional
Hamburg fish dishes. Ask for a window seat to enjoy the views over
the Nikolaifleet back towards town. ⓐ Deichstrasse 43 ❶ (040) 36 29 90
Ⓦ www.aalspeicher.de ❷ 12.00–24.00 ❸ U-bahn: U3 to Rödingsmarkt

Casse Croûte ££ ⓭ Bistro near the Opera House, with welcoming
white tablecloths and gleaming glassware, suitable both for lunch
or for a candlelit meal of an evening. Serves traditional German
dishes "from Grandmother's cookery book" as well as francophile
bistro fare. ⓐ Büschstrasse 2 ❶ (040) 34 33 73 ❶ (040) 358 96 50
Ⓦ www.cassecroute.de ❷ 12.00–24.00 Mon–Sat, 17.00–24.00 Sun
❸ U-bahn: U2 to Gänsemarkt

Fillet of Soul ££ ⓮ Trendy young German cuisine in the Deichtorhallen.
Floor-to-ceiling windows, open kitchen, modern décor. Can get very
busy at lunchtime, so it might be worth your while waiting for the
evening serving (from 18.00). On sunny days eat outside on the

terrace. ⓐ Deichtorstrasse 2 ⓣ (040) 7070 58 00 ⓦ www.fillet-of-soul.de ⓛ 11.00–22:00 Tues–Sun ⓝ U-bahn: U1 to Steinstrasse

Galatea ££ ⓯ Classy Italian restaurant, romantically housed in a boat on the Binnenalster. Great views across the lake, especially at twilight. Very popular with the evening theatre crowd. ⓐ Ballindamm ⓣ (040) 33 72 27 ⓛ 17.00–23.00 ⓝ all lines to Jungfernstieg

Old Commercial Room ££ ⓰ A traditional Hamburg favourite next to the Michaeliskirche. The interior is nautically themed and old-fashioned and the menu is unexciting but always reliable. It claims to be the best place in town for *Labskaus* (see pages 24–5). ⓐ Englische Planke 10 ⓣ (040) 36 63 19 ⓦ www.oldcommercialroom.de ⓛ 12.00–24.00 ⓝ U-bahn:U3 to Rödingsmarkt; Bus: 37 to Michaeliskirche

Parlament ££ ⓱ Downstairs in the Rathaus, modern design in an historic setting under painted vaulted ceilings. German food with a modern touch, lunchtime specials, very friendly and helpful staff. Can get very full at lunchtime. More seating outside on the Rathausmarkt, and also on the exquisite courtyard square behind the Rathaus. Cocktail hour from 22.00. ⓐ Rathausmarkt 1 ⓣ (040) 70 38 33 99 ⓦ www.parlament-hamburg.de ⓛ 11.00–00.00 Mon, 11.00–01.00 Wed–Thur, 11.00–late Fri & Sat, 09.30–23.00 Sun ⓝ U-bahn: U3 to Rathaus

Restaurant Schifferbörse ££ ⓲ Depending on your tastes, this restaurant is either enticingly maritime or absolutely OTT, being completely decked out in nautical props from various TV and film productions. The décor does not, however, distract from the excellence

of the fish dishes on offer. ⓐ Kirchenallee 46 ⓣ (040) 245 240
ⓛ 11.30–23.30 ⓝ all lines to Hauptbahnhof

Saliba ££ ⓱ Excellent Syrian and Lebanese food is served in this cosy
little candlelit restaurant in the Alsterarkaden. The *mezes* (hors d'oeuvres)
alone are a feast. There is a larger, very popular branch in Altona.
ⓐ Alsterarkaden, Neuer Wall 13 ⓣ (040) 34 50 21 ⓦ www.saliba.de
ⓛ 11.00–23.00 (last orders 22.00) ⓝ all lines to Jungfernstieg

Krameramtstuben am Michel £££ ⓴ Entering this almost
hidden world of tiny almshouses (see page 66) is a little bit like
stepping into a period film set, or even a giant doll's house, and
the authentic local cooking makes this a quintessential old-world
Hamburg experience. There are lots of different rooms so look

🔺 *Riverside dining is a perfect way to end the day*

GOOD AREAS FOR BARS

The best area in the city centre for a bar crawl is Grossneumarkt (**S**-Bahn: S1, S3 to Stadthausbrücke), where you'll also find a good choice of informal eating places. On summer nights the square is packed. Try Schwenders if you want an elegant café restaurant or Thämers for a cosy pub-style bar. Another popular area is Lange Reihe in the St Georg district, next to Hauptbahnhof. Café Gnosa at no. 93 has an interesting 1950s interior and caters for a mixed straight and gay crowd.

around if you are given the choice. **a** Krayenkamp 10 **t** 36 58 00 **w** www.krameramtsstuben.de **L** 12 .00–24.00 **N** U-bahn: U3 to Rödingsmarkt; Bus: 37 to Michaeliskirche

Plat du Jour £££ 21 Fine French bistro cooking aimed at the business community is on offer at this long-established Hamburg favourite but the eponymous plat du jour provides good value for budget-conscious visitors too. **a** Dornbusch 4 **t** (040) 32 14 14 **L** 12.00–22.30 Mon–Sat **N** U-bahn: U3 to Rathaus

BARS

Milk Bar Lounge Mellow lounge and cocktail bar right next to the entrance to Planten un Blomen park (directly opposite the Cinemaxx complex). The music is kept low enough that you can hear yourself talk, and you can sit outside on the deck in summer. Happy hour 18.00–22.00, snacks served 16.30–21.30 **a** Dammtordamm 2 **t** (040)348 00 34 **w** www.milkbarlounge.de **L** 14.00–late Mon, 15.00–late Tues–Fri, 13.00–late Sat & Sun **N** U-bahn: U1 to Stephansplatz

Nachtasyl Retro 60s bar upstairs in the Thalia Theatre. Great for just a drink (and mingling with theatre folk), but also occasional host to readings and concerts, in which case admission is charged at the door. One Saturday a month Hip Cat Club, beat and 60s soul disco (€5 admission on the door). Minimal bar snacks served. ❸ Alstertor 1 ❶ (040) 32 814 207 Ⓦ www.thalia-theater.de ❹ 19:00–late Tues–Sat Ⓝ all lines to Jungfernstieg

Nagel Friendly pub in prime position opposite the Hauptbahnhof, providing a haven for commuters and theatre-goers alike. Tasty food of the typically German fried potato variety, excellent beers on tap, great waiters! ❸ Kirchenallee 17 ❶ (040) 24 71 21 Ⓦ www.bodega–nagel.de ❹ 10.00–01.00 Sun–Thur, 10.00–02.00 Fri & Sat Ⓝ all lines to Hauptbahnhof

ENTERTAINMENT
Cotton Club Established in 1959, the Cotton Club stages live jazz and occasional blues with the emphasis on Dixieland hot jazz and swing. Intimate pub atmosphere, reasonable prices. ❸ Alter Steinweg 10 ❶ (040) 34 38 78 Ⓦ www.cotton-club.org ❹ doors open 20.00 Mon–Sat, 11.00–15.00 Sun Ⓝ S-bahn: S1, S3 to Stadthausbrücke; U-bahn: U3 to Rödingsmarkt

Hamburgische Staatsoper The Hamburg State Opera is ranked among the very best in the world and its ballet company has a high reputation, too. The Hamburg Philharmonic State Orchestra provides the music for most opera and ballet productions. ❸ Dammtorstrasse ❶ (040) 35 68 68 Ⓦ www.hamburgische-staatsoper.de Ⓝ U-bahn: U2 to Gänsemarkt; U1 to Stephansplatz

THE CITY

Hamburg harbour

Although most of the city's once-great shipbuilding industry has been lost to the Far East, the vast majority of goods that enter Germany today still pass through Hamburg, and as it has done for centuries, the port provides the city with its wealth. Depending on the definition of 'port', 'container port' or 'harbour', this is the largest or second-largest in Europe (after Rotterdam) and employs 155,000 people. It comprises 60 basins and around 45 km (27 miles) of quays. Around 300 shipping lines call here regularly to transport goods to and from 1000 ports all over the world. The *Landungsbrücken* (landing stages) on the harbour front, which float to allow for the tides (3.5 m/11 ft on average), are the longest of their kind in the world.

During World War II the harbour area was a key Allied target and very few buildings survived the bombing. The Speicherstadt (literally, 'warehouse town'), however, retains its history and there are a couple of notable small 17th-century enclaves in this area.

The U-Bahn runs along the harbour front on an elevated section of track between Baumwall and Landungsbrücken stations and is useful for continuing on to St Pauli and Reeperbahn stations, which service the Reeperbahn, St Pauli's main street.

SIGHTS & ATTRACTIONS

BallinStadt Museum Complex
Take a ride on the Maritime Circle Line to the southern side of the docks (HVV tickets are not valid for this service, which costs €5) and the BallinStadt Emigration City. This amazing 'Port of Dreams' museum experience is based on historical fact and is in a place of historical significance: this is the exact spot where thousands of

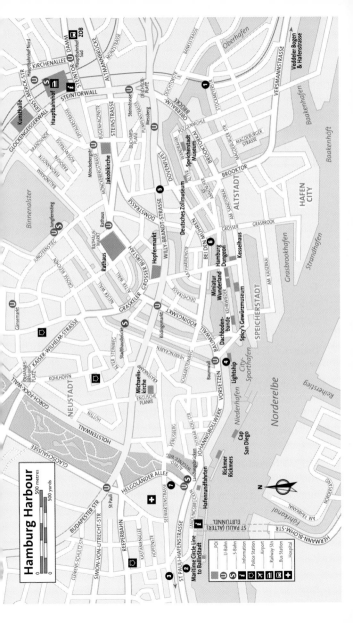

Hamburg Harbour

0 — 500 metres
0 — 500 yards

Binnenalster

Neustadt

St Pauli

Altstadt

Hafen City

Speicherstadt

Norderelbe

Baakenhöft

Oberhafen

Grasbrookhafen

Strandhafen

Reiherstieg

Veddeler Bogen & Hafenstrasse

Streets & Places

GLOCKENGIESSERWALL
ERNST-MERCK-STR
KIRCHENALLEE
STEINTORDAMM
MÜNZSTRASSE
BANKSTRASSE
STEINTORWALL
STEINTORWEG
STEINTOR
ALTMANNBRÜCKE
BRANDSENDE
FERDINANDSTOR
LANGE MÜHREN
DEICHTORPLATZ
OBERBAUM BRÜCKE
STOCKMEYER
VERSMANNSTRASSE
BRANDSTWIETE
BURCHARDPLATZ
MÖNCKEBERGSTR
MÖNCKEBERGSTRASSE
STEINSTRASSE
PUMPENSTRASSE
MESSBERG
POGGENMÜHLE
BROOKTORKAI
BRANDSTWIETE
DOVENFLEET
ALTER WANDRAHM
BROOKTOR
AM SANDTORKAI
GROSSER GRASBROOK
DOMSTRASSE
WILLY-BRANDT-STRASSE
GRASKELLER
GROSSER BURSTAH
BEI DEN MÜHREN
KEHRWIEDER
AM KAISERKAI
RATHAUSMARKT
ALTER WALL
GRASKELLER
RÖDINGSMARKT
HERRENGRABEN
SCHAARTENENG
KLEINE REICHENSTR
GROSSE REICHENSTR
BALLINDAMM
JUNGFERNSTIEG
NEUER WALL
GROSSE BLEICHEN
KAISER-WILHELM-STRASSE
JOHANNES-BRAHMS-PLATZ
ALTER STEINWEG
STADTHAUSBRÜCKE
NEUSTADT
KOHLHÖFEN
HOLSTENWALL
GORCH-FOCK-WALL
GLACISCHAUSSEE
BUDAPESTER STR
REEPERBAHN
SIMON-VON-UTRECHT-STR
CLEMENS-SCHULTZ-STR
KASTANIENALLEE
HOPFENSTR
ST PAULI-HAFENSTRASSE
HELGOLÄNDER ALLEE
SEEWARTENSTRASSE
ALFRED-WEGENER-WEG
BERNHARD-NOCHT-STR
LANDUNGSBRÜCKEN
JOHANNISBOLLWERK
VORSETZEN
BAUMWALL
STEINHÖFT
ENGLISCHE PLANKE
 VENUSBERG
DITMAR-KOEL-STR
HERRLICHKEIT
DECHSTRASSE
CREMON
HOHE BRÜCKE
KAJEN
BEIM ALTEN WAISENHAUSE
HERMANN-BLOHM-STR
ST PAULI (ALTER) ELBTUNNEL
AM ELBKANAL

Sights & Attractions

1. Speicherstadt Museum
2. Hamburg Dungeon
3. Miniatur Wunderland
4. Spicy's Gewürzmuseum
5. Deutsches Zollmuseum

Kunsthalle
Hauptbahnhof
Jakobikirche
Rathaus
Hopfenmarkt
Kesselhaus
Dachbodenbande
Michaeliskirche
Cap San Diego
Rickmer Rickmers
Lightship
City-Sporthafen
Niederhafen
Gänsemarkt

Legend

- POI
- U-Bahn
- S-Bahn
- Information
- Police Station
- Airport
- Railway Stn
- Bus Station
- Hospital

Maritime Circle Line to BallinStadt
Hafenrundfahrten

N

Europeans left in the hope of a better life in the New World. On top
of exhibits including passenger lists from 1850 to 1934, the buildings
of the time have been reconstructed to show how people lived while
waiting for their passage. Original cobblestones were integrated
into the complex, enabling visitors to literally tread the same path
as their forefathers on their way through the exhibition. State-of-
the-art media installations abound, including 'talking' mannequins,
videos and film clips. The interactive elements are designed to awake
an emotional reaction as visitors embark upon a trip of their own
through all major stages of emigration. The museum also incorporates
a family research centre with trained staff to help you research
the history of your own family. Drop in on the Hafenmuseum
(harbour museum) on your way back to town. ❸ Veddeler Bogen 2
❶ (040) 3197 91 60 ⓦ www.ballinstadt.de ⏰ 10.00–18.00 Ⓝ S-bahn:
S3, S31 to Veddel; Maritime Circle Line departs Landungsbrücken ten
every two hours 10.00–18.00. Admission charge

Deutsches Zollmuseum (German Customs Museum)
The former customs post is now a museum illustrating the difficulties
of preventing theft, smuggling and counterfeit goods through
the ages: some really wonderful exhibits. ❸ Alter Wandrahm 16
❶ (040) 300 876 11 ⓦ www.museum.zoll.de ⏰ 10.00–17.00 Tues–Sun
Ⓝ U-bahn: U1 to Messberg

Die Dachbodenbande (Toy Museum)
Two hundred years' worth of toys is the theme of this charming little
museum. Take a tour by torchlight in winter months. ❸ Kehrwieder 4
❶ 0172 329 3250 ⓦ www.dachbodenbande.de ⏰ 10.00–18.00
Ⓝ U-bahn: U3 to Baumwall. Admission charge

HafenCity

In the empty docklands area that lies beyond the Speicherstad
a whole new 'Harbour City' is taking shape, the biggest project of
its kind in Europe. A former boiler house, the Kesselhaus, has been
converted into the HafenCity InfoCenter, featuring a large-scale
model and various exhibits. ❸ Am Sandtorkai 30 ❶ (040) 36 90 17 99
Ⓦ www.HafenCity.com 🕐 10.00–18.00 Tues–Sun Ⓝ U-bahn: U3
to Baumwall

Hafenrundfahrten (Harbour tours)

There are three kinds of tour: around the harbour, around the
canals of the Speicherstadt or a combination of the two. Just the
harbour or just the canals take around an hour. There is only one
regular English-language harbour tour available to the general
public (i.e. without a group booking). This leaves daily at noon,
March to November, from the Landungsbrücken, Brücke (pier) 1
(❶ (040) 31 78 22 31).

Some single-decker cruisers combine the harbour and the
canals, though these are not as comfortable as the larger ships and
few offer English-language commentaries. One that does occasional
tours in English is Elbe-und Hafentouristik Glitscher at Brücke 6, 7
❶ (040) 737 4343 Ⓦ www.glitscher-hamburg.de). You can buy tickets
for all harbour cruises at the tourist office and ask them about
English-language tours.

Hamburg Dungeon

Hamburg's horrible history is depicted here in all its gruesome
gore, including the execution of the feared pirate Störtebeker
and 70 of his companions, and death and destruction in the
Great Fire of Hamburg. Not for the fainthearted or young children

but teens love it. ⓐ Kehrwieder 2, Block D ❶ (040) 36 00 55 20
ⓦ www.hamburgdungeon.com ❶ 11.00–18.00 Ⓝ U-bahn:
U3 to Baumwall. Admission charge

Miniatur Wunderland

This is the largest H0-Gauge model railroad layout in the world,
comprising more than 1,000 trains hauling over 15,000 carriages
around models of Hamburg, Scandinavia, the Florida Keys and lots
more national and international mini-landscapes. You can be part
of the action, pushing buttons so that a mine train starts, a shark
chases a diver, 'GOAL!!!' sounds from the Hamburg HSH Nordbank
football stadium, and so on. Every few minutes the main lights
dim, and around 200,000 tiny bulbs illuminate this engaging
little world. ⓐ Kehrwieder 2 ❶ (040) 300 68 00 ⓦ www.miniatur-
wunderland.de ❶ 09.30–18.00 Mon & Wed–Fri, 09.30–21.00 Tues,
08.00–21.00 Sat, 08.30–20.00 Sun & holidays Ⓝ U-bahn: U3 to
Baumwall. Admission charge

Rickmer Rickmers

Named after the son of the owner – his cherubic face smiles down
from the ship's figurehead – this former East Indies windjammer
dates from 1896, and was one of the last three-masted sailing ships
to be built in Germany. The *Rickmer Rickmers* sailed the oceans of
the world for 66 years and could carry loads of up to 3,000 tons
with a crew of just 24, who would be away from shore for up to
five months at a time. It is now a museum; areas open to visitors
include the engine room, the crew's quarters and galleys, and there
are special exhibitions. The ship is also home to an attractive
restaurant. A second museum ship, the *Cap San Diego*, is moored
alongside. ⓐ Ponton 1A, Landungsbrücken ❶ (040) 319 59 59

○ *Herr Rickmers' son stares out from his father's ship*

ⓦ www.rickmer-rickmers.de ⓛ 10.00–18.00 ⓝ U-bahn: U3;
S-bahn: S1, S3 to Landungsbrücken. Admission charge

Speicherstadt

The typically Hanseatic dark-red brick Speicherstadt is the biggest
warehouse complex in the world, with 373,000 sq m (447,000 sq yd)
of storage space housing such valuable goods as coffee, tea, tobacco,
spices, alcoholic drinks, oriental carpets and silks. Under the privileges
granted to the port they may be stored duty-free for as long as their
owners wish before they are sold – usually when market prices rise
to a sufficiently tempting price.

The Speicherstadt was built between 1855 and 1910. Around half
of it was destroyed during the war but it has been subsequently
restored and the buildings are protected, so even today you will see
old-fashioned mechanical hoists being used, as modern lifts cannot
be installed. The Speicherstadt incorporates some good museums –
the Deutsches Zollmuseum (see page 90), Speicherstadt Museum
and Spicy's Gewürzmuseum (see page 95).

At the western end of the Speicherstadt (towards the harbour),
the Kehrwiedersteg bridge crosses the water back towards the city
into Deichstrasse. Some of the city's oldest and most picturesque
buildings, dating back to the 17th century, lie along here. At the back
of the houses is the Nikolaifleet canal, and on the other side, on the
street known as Cremon, are also several historic, photogenic houses.
Several have been turned into places to eat and drink.

Speicherstadt Museum

This atmospheric little display is a logical introduction to the
Speicherstadt, even if the exhibits, such as typical tools and samples
of goods, are workaday. Warning: to reach the museum you have to

climb three floors of creaking stairs. If you are interested in a guided tour, phone the museum and they will try and get an English-speaking group together. ❸ St Annenufer 2, Block R ❶ (040) 32 11 91 ❿ www.speicherstadtmuseum.de ❺ 10.00–17.00 Tues–Sun (also Mon on public hols) ❻ U-bahn: U1 to Messberg. Admission charge

Spicy's Gewürzmuseum

'The hottest admission ticket in town' (a packet of black peppercorns, which you get to keep as your entrance receipt) sets the tone for this very likeable trawl through the world of spices. All captions are in perfect English, your knowledge is tested en route and perhaps most enjoyable of all are the many old-fashioned examples of packaging and advertising memorabilia and curiosities from around the world, such as the model ship from Indonesia made entirely from cloves. ❸ Am Sandtorkai 32, Block L, 2nd floor ❶ (040) 36 79 89 ❿ www.spicys.de ❺ 10.00–17.00 Tues–Sun ❻ U-bahn:U3 to Baumwall. Admission charge

TAKING A BREAK

Many of the little *Kajüte* (cabins) on the Landungsbrücken serve good quality fish rolls to take away or eat in, as well as inexpensive fish meals.

Oberhafenkantine £ ❶ A crooked little house under a railway bridge round the back of the Speicherstadt, run by the mother of a famous TV chef. Not only is this an architectural gem and important historical landmark, it is a temple of good home cooking and excellent value for money. ❸ Stockmeyerstrasse 39 ❿ www.oberhafenkantine.de

🕐 11.30–15.00, 17.00–22.00 (15.00–17.00 only cold food available)
Mon–Sat Ⓜ U-bahn: U1 to Messberg

Beach clubs ££ ❷ & ❸ In the chill of midwinter it's hard to believe
this is possible and even in season there's something a little bit
tongue-in-cheek about the whole thing, but from May to the end
of September beach life is re-created (as far as that is possible
when it is 15°C (59°F) and raining outside) on the banks of the
Elbe by a number of 'beach clubs'. Colonial furniture, decking, deck
chairs, potted palms, chill-out music, tropical cocktails, barbecues,
even beach volleyball on brought-in white sand, all helps creates
the illusion of exotic climes. All open at noon and stay open late.
The nearest one to town is StrandPauli (Ⓐ Hafenstrasse 89
Ⓦ www.strandpauli.de), in between the Landungsbrücken and
the Fischmarkt. A little further downriver are Hamburg City Beach
Club, (Ⓦ www.hamburgcitybeachclub.de), Lago Bay (Ⓦ www.lago.cc)
and Hamburg del Mar (Ⓦ www.hamburg-del-mar.de), Ⓐ all Van-der-
Smissen-Strasse Ⓝ S-bahn: S1, S3 to Königstrasse; Water bus: 86 to
Dockland landing stage

Feuerschiff (Lightship) ££ ❹ It's worth popping on board if only to
see inside this bright red lighthouse ship (built in England) and you
can enjoy a coffee, a beer, a snack or a full meal at any time of the
day. It is at its best, however, on Sunday lunchtime or Monday
evening, when a jazz band plays. The busy low-ceilinged interior,
with its multi-levels, makes a perfect setting and there's a friendly,
lively atmosphere. Ⓐ Vorsetzen, City Sporthafen 🕿 (040) 36 25 53
Ⓦ www.das-feuerschiff.de 🕐 Bar: 11.00–13.00 Mon–Sat,

◀ *The Lightship is an unmissable sight on Hamburg's waterfront*

THE CITY

10.00–22.30 Sun; Restaurant: 12.00–22.00 Mon–Sat, 10.00–17.00 Sun; Jazz: 11.00–14.40 Sun, from 20.30 onwards Mon Ⓝ U-bahn: U3 to Baumwall. Admission charge for Sunday jazz sessions

AFTER DARK

Gröninger Braukeller & Brauhaus Hanseat Dehns Privatbrauerei £ ❺
This Braukeller in the south of the old town has been brewing on the premises since 1750. A good-time bar with *Wurst und Kartoffeln* (sausage and potatoes) to soak up the copious quantities of home-brewed beer that are drunk here. Go with a group to get the best out of it. ⓐ Willy-Brandt-Strasse 47 ❶ (040) 33 13 81 ⓦ www.groeninger-hamburg.de ⓛ 11.00–late Mon–Fri, 17.00–late Sat Ⓝ U-bahn: U1 to Messberg

Brook ££ ❻ Family-run upmarket restaurant, very stylish but still comfortable. Wonderful food plus view of the Speicherstadt. If you want to treat yourself to a special meal on the last evening of your holiday, this is the place to do it. ⓐ Bei den Mühren 91 ❶ (040) 37 50 31 ⓛ 12.00–15.00, 18.00–22.30 Mon–Sat Ⓝ U-bahn: U3 to Rödingsmarkt

The Tower Bar ££ ❼ Located right on top of the landmark Hafen Hotel, this offers easily the best view of the area by night, with the port to one side and the spectacular lights of the Dom funfair (when it is there) to the other. Start your night off here with a Happy Hour drink. ⓐ Seewartenstrasse 9 ❶ (040) 31 11 30 ⓦ `www.hotel-hafen-hamburg.de ⓛ 18.00–02.00 (Happy Hour 18.00–19.00) Ⓝ S-bahn: S1, S3; U-bahn: U3 to Landungsbrücken

⬧ *The harbour glows at night*

North of the centre

Aside from visiting the Aussenalster lake, most short-stay visitors to Hamburg don't venture north of the old city wall boundary – which is a shame, particularly in good weather, because just beyond is the lovely northern section of the Planten un Blomen gardens, one of the world's best zoos, and around the lakeside, beautiful parkland with cafés and restaurants frequented by well-heeled locals at the weekend.

For the location of places mentioned in this chapter, see the main city map, pages 52–3.

● *Planten un Blomen is Hamburg's green heart*

SIGHTS & ATTRACTIONS

Hagenbeck Tierpark (Hagenbeck's Zoo)

Established in 1907, Hagenbeck's is one of the world's leading zoos and pioneered the principle of keeping animals in near-natural enclosures without cages. Today it is home to around 2,500 animals representing 360 species, many of which are housed in the 56 open-air spaces. The park is beautifully landscaped with lakes and crags and botanical gardens with rare plants.

   In summer the zoo stages a series of special evenings on some Saturday nights (small additional charge). *Jungle Nights*, featuring exotic music and entertainment, runs from mid-May to early June, while *Romantic Nights* in August brings live classical music.
ⓐ Lokstedter Grenzstrasse 2 ❶ (040) 53 00 330 ❶ (040) 53 00 33 341
ⓦ www.hagenbeck.de ⓛ 09.00–17.00 (19.00 if weather permits)
mid-Mar–Oct; 09.00–16.30 Nov–mid-Mar ⓝ U-bahn: U2 to
Hagenbecks Tierpark. Admission charge

Hagenbeck Tropen-Aquarium

Hamburg's first and only large-scale aquarium! Three levels over 8,000 sq m (86,111 sq ft): deep tropical oceans, subtropical rainforest and the secret subterannean world of caves and grottoes. Biodiversity is the keyword here, with different species sharing the same territory just as they would in the wild. See the creatures close up in conditions as close to their natural surroundings as was possible to recreate, on land, in water or under the earth. The aquarium is dedicated to the protection of endangered species. A combination ticket for aquarium and zoo is available. ⓐ Lokstedter Grenzstrasse 2
❶ (040) 53 00 330 ❶ (040) 53 00 33 341 ⓦ www.hagenbeck.de

(follow the links to Tropen-Aquarium) 🕐 09.00–18.00 Ⓝ U-bahn:
U2 to Hagenbecks Tierpark. Admission charge

Museum für Völkerkunde (Ethnological Museum)

Hamburg's most exotic museum is a treasure chest of souvenirs
collected by merchants and seafarers from Africa, Asia, America,
Oceania and the more far-flung corners of Europe, ever since its
inception in 1879. These range in size from moccasins from North
America to a full-scale Maori Meeting Hall. The masks from Oceania
are a favourite. 🖈 Rothenbaumchaussee 64 🕐 01805 30 88 88
🌐 www.voelkerkundemuseum.com 🕐 10.00–18.00 Tues–Sun,
10.00–21.00 Thur, closed Mon Ⓝ U-bahn: U1 to Hallerstrasse;
S-bahn:S21, S31 to Dammtor. Admission charge

Planetarium Hamburg

Located just beyond the northern tip of the Aussenalster in the
Stadtpark, this is one of the most advanced planetariums in the
world. The commentary is only in German but you won't need
words to appreciate the state-of-the-art cosmos simulator,
Digistar 3, which takes visitors on a three-dimensional journey
over millions of light years in *Eternal Worlds – from the Big Bang
to Planet Earth*, witnessing the life and death of stars and galaxies.

While you are waiting for the show, there's a window on the
universe via large format high-resolution plasma screens linked online
to the Hubble Space Telescope. If you want more down-to-earth views
after all that, step up to the Observation Deck, which at a mere 50 m
(164 ft) offers a fine panorama of the city with the Aussenalster in
the foreground.

Music fans might also like to check out the Planetarium programme,
which features special shows such as *Dark Side of The Moon*,

△ *Planetarium, Hamburg's best spot for star-gazing*

to the eponymous Pink Floyd album soundtrack, *The Cosmic Wall
– A Monument to Pink Floyd*, *Aero* by Jean Michel Jarre, and *Deep
Space Night*, which mixes classical, pop, rock and trance music. Live
concerts and laser shows are also staged here. ❸ Hindenburgstrasse,
Stadtpark ❶ (040) 428 86 52 10 Ⓦ www.planetarium-hamburg.de
🕐 09.00–15.00 Tues, 09.00–21.00 Wed, 09.00–21.30 Thur,
09.00–21.45 Fri, 12.30–21.30 Sat, 12.30–19.00 Sun Ⓝ U-bahn:
U3 to Borgweg. Admission charge

Planten un Blomen

The largest city park, Planten un Blomen is part of a green belt that stretches north from the St Pauli U-Bahn station and the Hamburg History Museum (see pages 67–8) as far as the landmark *Fernsehturm* (television tower) The southern section includes crazy golf, trampolines and a roller-skating rink (converted to ice-skating in winter). The northern half is more decorative, though it too includes a large children's play area with water effects and pony rides on Sundays. Adults are more likely to enjoy the Planten un Blumen botanical gardens, including an apothecaries' garden, a rose garden, a tropical greenhouse and Europe's largest Japanese Garden. This includes a tea house where special exhibitions on aspects of Oriental culture are held and the tea ceremony is demonstrated. Also in the northern section, on summer nights, fountains illuminated by coloured lights dance in the lake; the dancing fountains also 'perform' without lights at 14.00, 16.00, 18.00 on a daily basis; on Sundays and holidays recorded music is added to the 14.00 performance. There are free concerts in the music pavilion, ranging from tango or rock'n'roll to big-band jazz, mostly on weekend afternoons. Ⓦ www.plantenunblomen.hamburg.de Ⓛ 07.00–23.00 May–Sept; 07.00–20.00 Oct–Apr; Illuminated fountains

---

HERE ON BUSINESS?

Then you may well be heading to the Planten un Blomen park which is home to not only Hamburg's largest trade fairs and conventions centre, the Messe Hallen, but also the Congress Zentrum Hamburg (Hamburg Messe und Congress). This is one of the largest congress centres in the world, with seating for up to 10,000 delegates (Ⓦ www.hamburg-messe.de).

and concerts: 22.00 May–Aug; 21.00 Sept; Tea House: 15.00 Sun,
May–Sept Tropical greenhouse: 09.00–16.45 Mon–Fri, 10.00–17.45
Sat & Sun, Mar–Oct; 09.00–15.45 Mon–Fri, 10.00–15.45 Sat & Sun,
Nov–Feb ⓝ S-bahn: S 21, S31 to Dammtor; U-bahn: U1 to Stephansplatz,
U2 to Messehallen, U3 to St Pauli. Admission free to all areas except
mini-golf and trampolines

RETAIL THERAPY

The northern part of the city was, until recently, a bit of a shopping
desert. Now, though, Marktstrasse in the Karolinenviertel has become
a great place to head for hip fashions and quirky shops. Stretching from
Messehallen station ⓝ U-bahn: U2, to Feldstrasse tube ⓝ U-bahn: U3,
you'll find boutique upon boutique of streetware, vintage shops,
accessories, second-hand shops and young German designers.

Elternhaus does a very natty line in cult Maegde und Knechte
shirts and accessories. ⓐ Marktstrasse 29 ⓣ (040) 430 88 30
ⓛ 12.00–19.00 Mon–Fri, 11.00–19.00 Sat

Herr von Eden specialises in high-class couture for men
(ⓐ Marktstrasse 33, ⓣ (040) 439 00 57 ⓦ www.herrvoneden.com
ⓛ 11.00–20.00 Mon–Fri, 11.00–18.00 Sat). It also has an outlet shop
on the neighbouring Neustadt, where previous collections are sold
off at half price (ⓐ Kohlhöfen 8 ⓣ (040) 359 600 910 ⓛ 12.00–20.00
Mon–Fri, 12.00–18.00 Sat ⓝ U-bahn: U2 to Messehallen).

Wild One You don't have to be noticeably untamed to shop in this
modest emporium that specialises in Hamburg streetware.
ⓐ Marktstrasse 100 ⓣⓕ (040) 439 21 16

TAKING A BREAK

Café Schöne Aussichten £ ❶ In the northern section of the Planten un Blomen park, this café lives up to its name with 'beautiful views' from its shady terrace. It is very popular in summer and serves until late into the evening to the sounds of house and soul music. ⓐ Gorch-Fock Wall 1 ❶ (040) 34 01 13 ⓛ 10.00–24.00 Sun–Thur; 10.00–02.00 Fri & Sat Ⓝ S-bahn: S21, S31 to Dammtor ❶ After Work Club, 18.00–24.00 Thur. Admission charge

Eisdealer £ ❷ Stop for an ice cream at Hamburg's hippest ice cream parlour, but don't expect to be served a Knickerbocker Glory. Mix and match from over 50 flavours, including some you'd never dreamed of. Try yoghurt ice cream with basil and toasted pine nuts or chocolate ice cream with red wine and chili. ⓐ Bartelsstrasse 8 ⓛ 12.00–22.00 Mon–Sat, 13.00–20.00 Sun Ⓝ U-bahn: U3; S-bahn: S21, S31 to Sternschanze

Schanzenstern £ ❸ Restaurant affilated with the Schanzenstern eco-hotel in Schanzenviertel, just north of the city centre. All produce organic, lunchtime menu 100 per cent vegetarian, more choice evenings. Popular brunch location Sundays. Peaceful green courtyard for al fresco dining. ⓐ Bartelsstrasse 12 ❶ (040) 432 904 09 ⓦ www.schanzenstern.de ⓛ 15.00–01.00 Mon, 10.30–01.00 Tues–Sat, 11.00–24.00 Sun, closed Mon lunchtime Ⓝ S-bahn: S21, S31; U-bahn:, U3 to Sternschanze

AFTER DARK

Hamburg University is located immediately north of the Planten un Blomen gardens and its presence ensures a number of lively bars in the area; Grindelallee in particular is heaving with cafés. For the best nightlife, however, you'll have to go immediately west to the Schanzenviertel, between St Pauli and Eimsbüttel. When the weather's nice, the scene moves onto the streets, especially on Schulterblatt.

RESTAURANTS

Restaurant Nil ££ ❹ On the edge of the St Pauli district, this classy retro-modern restaurant (housed in a beautiful old building) is one of the most talked about and popular places in town, serving excellent New German cuisine. Reservations essential; book a table in the gallery if possible. Come with plenty of cash, as credit cards are not accepted. ⓐ Neuer Pferdemarkt 5 ❶ (040) 439 78 23 ⓦ www.restaurant-nil.de ❶ 18.00–23.00 Mon, Wed & Thur, 18.00–24.00 Fri & Sat, 18.00–22.00 Sun, bar open until 02.00 Ⓝ U-bahn: U3 to Feldstrasse

BARS & CLUBS

Astra Stube Something of a cult venue, with an eclectic music line-up including punk rock, electro, reggae and pop. ⓐ Max-Brauer-Allee 200/ Stresemannstrasse ❶ (040) 43 25 06 26 ⓦ www.astrastube.de ❶ from 22.00 Fri & Sat Ⓝ Bus: 115 to Sternbrücke

Bar Rossi A popular meeting place for Hamburg's young trendies to see and be seen. You can prop up the retro-style bar, chill out on one of the plush sofas, groove to the sounds of drum and bass on a small dance floor or simply gaze out through the large windows at the city by night. ⓐ Max-Brauer-Allee 279 ❶ (040) 43 25 46 39 ❶ 18.00–03.00 Sun–Fri, 18.00–04.00 Sat Ⓝ U-bahn: U3; S-bahn: S21, S31 to Sternschanze; Bus: 115 to Schulterblatt

Die Welt ist Schön 'The World is Beautiful', and so are the people who frequent this stylish modern haunt on three floors, with roof

terrace, beer garden and dance floor. ⓐ Neuer Pferdemarkt 4
ⓣ (040) 401878 88 ⓦ www.dieweltistschoen.net ⓛ from 20.00
ⓝ U-bahn: U3 to Feldstrasse

Live Dark but comfortable bar, small enough for an intimate
atmosphere, offering a range of music styles throughout the week.
No admission charge for regular sessions, such as jazz on Tues evenings,
or on rare evenings with no live music on offer ⓐ Fruchtallee 36
ⓣ (040) 401 55 00 ⓦ www.music-club-live.de ⓛ bar open 18.00, music
from 21.00 Mon–Sat. Admission charge ⓝ U-bahn: U2 to Christuskirche

Uebel und Gefährlich Cutting-edge club on the top floor of the
Feldstrasse bunker – take the lift to the top. Indie/electro dance clubs,
but also concert gigs. Opening times vary enormously, so please consult
local press. ⓐ Feldstrasse 66 ⓦ www.uebelundgafährlich.com
ⓝ U-bahn:U3 to Feldstrasse

CLASSICAL MUSIC VENUES
Hochschüle für Musik und Theater
By the shores of the Alster, Hamburg's music academy stages
regular concerts by established musicians as well as from the
ranks of its own very talented students. ⓐ Harvestehuder Weg 12
ⓣ (040) 42 84 80 ⓝ U-bahn: U1 to Hallerstrasse.

Laeiszhalle/Musikhalle
This is one of the most beautiful concert venues in Germany,
with three halls offering a choice of orchestral, chamber, vocal
and instrumental concerts, and sometimes popular music or jazz.
ⓐ Johannnes-Brahms-Platz ⓣ (040) 34 69 20 ⓦ www.musikhalle-
hamburg.de ⓝ U-Bahn: U2 to Messehallen

⬥ *The Alster is a favourite spot for unwinding in the evening*

St Pauli & Altona

Where there's a port there is of course always a red-light district. Hamburg's lies just beyond the docks in the area of St Pauli. Once notorious, it is now well regulated and large parts of it have been transformed into the city's leading nightlife area with numerous theatres and respectable nightspots.

If you are only spending a couple of days in Hamburg you may not even hear the name Altona, let alone visit it. However, the two-hour sightseeing bus trip to Blankenese (see pages 124–9) may give you an idea of the area as it cruises along the grand Elbchaussee riverfront road.

Altona sits beside St Pauli, though they make unlikely neighbours, from raucous red-light district to leafy executive suburbia in just a couple of miles. Just west of the railway station Altona merges into Ottensen, and it is here that many of this area's more interesting shops, bars and restaurants are to be found.

SIGHTS & ATTRACTIONS

Dom

The huge Dom funfair sets up next to St Pauli station for around a month at a time each spring, summer and winter. It has been coming here for over a century and its roller-coasters and big wheel have become a part of the St Pauli skyline. In the wintertime (weather permitting) it also exhibits ice and snow sculptures. Fireworks every Friday evening (22.00). Wednesday is Family Day, with concessions on most rides. The fair remains shut on Good Friday. ⓐ Heiligengeistfeld, St Pauli ⓦ www.hamburger-dom.de ⓛ 15.00–23.00 Mon–Thur,

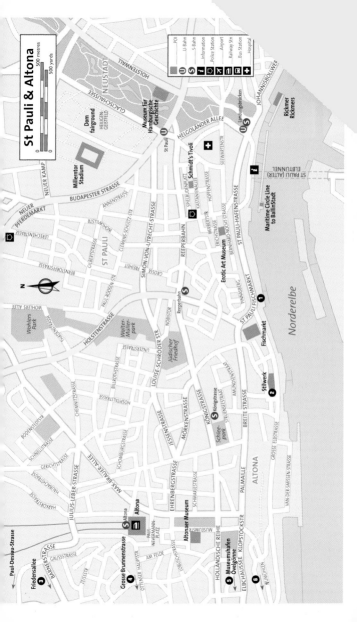

St Pauli & Altona

0 — 500 metres
0 — 500 yards

POI
U-Bahn
S-Bahn
Information
Police Station
Airport
Railway Stn
Bus Station
Hospital

N

HOLSTENWALL

NEUSTADT

GLACISCHAUSSEE

Dom
fairground

HEILIGEN-
GEISTFELD

Museum für
Hamburgische
Geschichte

Millerntor
Stadium

BUDAPESTER STRASSE

HELGOLÄNDER ALLEE

St Pauli

NEUER KAMP

NEUER
PFERDEMARKT

ANNENSTRASSE

Schmidt's Tivoli

SPIELBUDENPLATZ

KASTANIENALLEE

SEEWARTENSTR

KLEINE FREIHEIT

GILBERTSTRASSE

PAUL ROOSEN STR

ST PAULI

SIMON-VON-UTRECHT-STRASSE

HOPFENSTRASSE

HERBERTSTR

ERICHSTRASSE

BERNHARD-NOCHT-STRASSE

ST PAULI-HAFENSTRASSE

REEPERBAHN

Reeperbahn

GROSSE FREIHEIT

NOBISTOR

Erotic Art Museum

PANNBERG

ST PAULI FISCHMARKT

ST PAULI (ALTER)
ELBTUNNEL

JOHANNISBOLLWERK

Landungsbrücken

Rickmer
Rickmers

Maritime Circle Line
to BallinStadt

Norderelbe

BERNSTORFFSTRASSE

LERCHENSTRASSE

WOHLERS ALLEE

Wohlers
Park

HOLSTENSTRASSE

Walter-
Müller-
park

Jüdischer
Friedhof

LOUISE-SCHRÖDER-STR

UNZERSTRASSE

BILLROTHSTRASSE

HOSPITALSTRASSE

CHEMNITZSTRASSE

SCHOMBURGSTRASSE

JESSENSTRASSE

MÖRKENSTRASSE

KÖNIGSTRASSE

Königstrasse

STRUENSEESTR

AMUNDSENSTR

Schlee-
park

BREITE STRASSE

Stilwerk

Fischmarkt

BODENSTEDTSTR

SCHNELLSTRASSE

GERICHTSTRASSE

HÄLBACHSTRASSE

HARKORTSTRASSE

JULIUS-LEBER-STRASSE

MAX-BRAUER-ALLEE

EHRENBERGSTRASSE

SCHMARJESTR

PALMAILLE

GROSSE ELBSTRASSE

VAN-DER-SMISSEN-STRASSE

ALTONA

Paul-Dessau-Strasse

Friedensallee

BARNERSTRASSE

GAUSSSTRASSE

ZEISSTR

OTTENSER HAUPTSTR

AM FELDE

OELKERSSTRASSE

PAUL-
NEVERMANN-
PLATZ

Altona

Grosse Brunnenstrasse

Altonaer Museum

MUSEUMSTR

HOLLÄNDISCHE REIHE

ELBCHAUSSEE

KLOPSTOCKSTR

Museumshafen
Oevelgönne

NEUMÜHLEN

organises a number of guided walks which
…ects of the St Pauli area: *Merchants' Pride
and Sailors' Dreams* departs 11.00 Sunday and 15.00 Saturday
(Feb–late Nov) from Rathaus main entrance; *Pub Crawling on
the Reeperbahn* departs 20.00 Fri from Millentorplatz/St Pauli
U-Bahn (Feb–Nov); *Neon lights, Seedy Bars and Fervent Catholics
– a stroll through St Pauli* departs 15.00 Saturday from the clock
tower at Landungsbrücken (Feb–late Nov). *The Beatles in St Pauli
– a Magical Mystery Tour* departs 19.00 Saturday (May–late Sept)
from Feldstrasse U-Bahn. Note that all tours require booking
(at the tourist office) and are subject to minimum numbers
and availability of English-language guides.

15.00–24.00 (summer until 00.30) Fri & Sat, 14.00–23.00 Sun
Ⓝ U-bahn: U3 to Feldstrasse.

Erotic Art Museum

It's obviously not for the prudish (visitors must be 16 or older)
but neither is this just a glorified porn exhibition: many of
its exhibits are first-class works of art. In fact this is one of the
world's biggest collections of erotic art, with around 1,800 pieces
spanning 500 years. ⓐ Bernhard-Nocht-Strasse 69, St Pauli
ⓣ (040) 31 78 410 ⓦ www.eroticartmuseum.de ⓛ 12.00–22.00
Sun–Thur, 12.00–24.00 Fri & Sat Ⓝ U-bahn: U3;S-bahn: S1,
S3 to Landungsbrücken. Admission charge

Ⓞ *The Dom's big wheel is a colourful way to view Hamburg*

Fischmarkt (Fish Market)

A 300-year-old Hamburg institution, the Fischmarkt is as colourful a genuine street market as you will find in northern Europe and works on all levels for all people. Locals come here to pick up some astonishing bargains of exotic flowers, plants, fruits, vegetables, and, of course fish, from garrulous noisy stall holders; revellers come fresh off the Reeperbahn to extend their drinking and dancing; tourists come to browse for souvenirs, eat and drink at the dozens of refreshment stalls and listen to the music. The Fischmarkt hall, a striking cavernous steel and glass structure on two floors, is given over for the morning to eating, drinking and live bands who play jazz, pop and anything danceable. ⊕ St Pauli Fischmarkt ⊕ 05.00–10.00 Sun, summer; 07.00–10.00 Sun, winter ⊕ S-bahn: S1, S3 to Reeperbahn

Museumshafen Övelgönne (Museum Harbour)

One of Hamburg's quaintest attractions, this is a little basin housing a mixture of historical and interesting boats. Exhibits include barges, long boats, offshore fishing vessels, steam-driven tugs and a lightship, all of them working ships. There are plaques up on the bridge with information such as names, dates and home harbours, but crew members working on the boats will be glad to answer any questions or even invite you on board for a closer look. The museum harbour also houses an old ferry which has been converted to a café. ⊕ Övelgönne, Neumühlen landing stage ⊕ (040) 419 127 61 (office) ⊕ www.museumshafen-oevelgoenne.de ⊕ Bus: 112; Water bus: 62 to Neumühlen landing stage

RETAIL THERAPY

Unless porno mags, rubber underwear and 'marital aids' from the Reeperbahn, or cheap, nautically-themed souvenirs (the ubiquitous ship in a bottle) from the touristy kiosks on the Landungsbrücken are on your shopping list, you won't find much to buy in this part of the city. There is the city's most famous market, however, plus one or two unusual outlets that deal in the exotic wares that pass through the port.

Harry's Hamburger Hafenbasar

More of an ethnographic museum than a conventional shop, this is a fascinating mish-mash of weird and wonderful items (including masks, musical instruments, furniture, statues, jewellery, textiles and of course erotic art and objects) collected by Hamburg seafarers from all over the world. The excellent website includes pictures of many items for sale, so you can browse before visiting or shop on-line. ⓐ Erichstrasse 56, St Pauli ① (040) 31 24 82 Ⓦ www.hafenbasar.de Ⓛ 12.00–18.00 Tues–Sun Ⓝ U-bahn U3; S-bahn: S1, S3 to Landungsbrücken. Small admission charge refundable against purchases

AFTER DARK – ST PAULI

Nightlife on the Reeperbahn is a heady mix of variety shows, cabarets, live music venues, DJ bars, bars with lap-dancing and pole-dancing and tacky outlets showing sex videos (live sex shows have dwindled to just one or two outlets as a result of the easy availability of internet porn). Prostitutes are not allowed to solicit on the actual Reeperbahn, though they may do so off it, especially around Herbertstrasse. This is a short street that is closed off and chicaned by brick walls (so it's impossible to enter by accident) and, like Amsterdam's famous red light area, features scantily clad girls sitting in windows. No other women, nor men under 18, are allowed into the street and should they attempt to enter, risk a soaking at the entrance (courtesy of an unobtrusive first-floor guardian) followed by immediate ejection. If you are looking for live music head for Grosse Freiheit. The famous Star Club, where many rock legends of the 1960s, including The Beatles (see pages 12–13), cut their musical teeth has long gone, but top international bands and up–and–coming groups still play on this street.

RESTAURANTS

Fischerhaus ££ ❶ One of the area's favourite fish restaurants. Downstairs is traditional with old-fashioned dark wood fittings; upstairs is very modern with bleached wood and harbour views (book a window seat if possible), and a slightly more expensive menu. Wherever you sit you get the freshest possible fish.
ⓐ St Pauli Fischmarkt 14 ❶ (040) 31 40 53 Ⓦ www.restaurant-fischerhaus.de Ⓛ 11.00–23.00 Ⓝ U-bahn U3; S-bahn: S1, S3 to Landungsbrücken

Warsteiner Elbspeicher £££ ❷ Very attractive place right on the waterfront, where traditional and modern mix effortlessly; light and airy décor with bare brick walls and an interesting menu with classic and new fish dishes. It also has a bistro in similar style.
ⓐ Grosse Elbstrasse 39 ❶ (040) 38 22 42 Ⓦ www.warsteiner-elbspeicher.de Ⓛ 12.00–24.00 (last orders 22.00) Ⓝ U-bahn U3; S-bahn: S1, S3 to Landungsbrücken

BARS

Meanie Bar & Molotow Meanie Bar is ideal if you're a bit old for a disco and don't fancy clubbing it but you would like to drop into a trendy, welcoming, bohemian bar where the DJs really get off on a broad range of toe-tapping music all the way back to the 1960s (in fact they love the 60s here!). If you are tempted to shake your bootay, pop downstairs to Molotow, where they have different theme nights and live indie and punk-rock bands play. ❸ Spielbudenplatz 5 ❶ (040) 31 96 087 Meanie Bar; (040) 31 08 45 Molotow ❾ www.meaniebar.de; www.molotowclub.com ❿ Meanie Bar: 21.00–04.00; Molotow: 23.00–04.00 Fri & Sat ❾ U-bahn: U3 to St Pauli

Yakshi's Bar Gorgeous bar in one of Hamburg's newest designer hotels, attracting a super-trendy cosmopolitan crowd. ❸ East Hotel, Simon-Von-Utrecht-Strasse 31 ❶ (040) 30 99 30 ❾ www.east-hamburg.de ❿ 10.00–late ❾ U-bahn: U3 to St Pauli; S-bahn: S1, S3 to Reeperbahn

MUSIC BARS & CLUBS

China Lounge Very stylish club with an Oriental theme playing a sophisticated mix of soul, funk, rare grooves, big beats/bossa nova and electronic sounds. ❸ Nobistor 14, Reeperbahn ❶ (040) 31 97 66 22 ❾ www.china-lounge.de ❿ 23.00–0.400 Tues, Fri & Sat, 22.00–04.00 Thurs, closed Mon & Sun ❾ S-bahn: S1, S3 to Reeperbahn

Docks House, hip-hop, R&B, dance classics and chart toppers – if you can dance to it they will play it at this huge club, which attracts up to 1,200 guests at a time. Live bands and go-go dancers too. ❸ Spielbudenplatz 19 ❶ (040) 31 78 83 0 ❾ www.docks.de ❿ 22.00 onwards Fri & Sat; for other nights, see website

Funky Pussy Club Very popular with Hamburg students, whose art academy helped design the club. R&B, hip-hop and dance classics. Every Thursday is College Night, with very cheap drinks. Hip-hop,

R&B, soul and house wth Latin dance tunes on Saturdays.
ⓐ Grosse Freiheit 34 ❶ (040) 31 42 36 ⓦ www.funkypussyclub.de
🕐 23.00–04.00 Thur–Sat ⓝ S-bahn: S1, S3 to Reeperbahn

Golden Pudel Club A well-established fixture on the Hamburg
scene, this harbourside club attracts live-music fans of all creeds
and is quick to pick up the latest trends. There's something
different on every night, so look at the programme on the
web or in *Pur* magazine (see page 29). ⓐ St Pauli Fischmarkt 27
❶ (040) 31 95 33 6 ⓦ www.pudel.com 🕐 22.00–04.00 ⓝ S-bahn:
S1, S3 to Reeperbahn

Grosse Freiheit 36 This is the main rock venue in town with big-name bands playing regularly. The Kaiserkeller downstairs is the setting for theme parties, usually rock-oriented but with exceptions such as reggae (Tues) and even psychedelic and garage. ② Grosse Freiheit 36 ❶ (040) 31 77 78 11 Ⓦ www.grossefreiheit36.de ❻ from 20.00 Mon, from 22.00 Tues–Sun Ⓢ S-bahn: S1, S3 to Reeperbahn

Halo This popular place made its name as the Betty Ford Klinik and some of Hamburg's top DJs make sure partygoers still get a first-

⬇ *Neon overload in lively Grosse Freiheit*

Hamburg and particularly the Reeperbahn is famous throughout
Germany for its cabaret and music-hall shows – the best known
being Schmidt's Tivoli. However unless you speak very good
German and can pick up topical humorous references, and
German slang, most of the show will go straight over your
head. Similarly, Hamburg's musicals are in German only. Its
latest offering, *Dirty Dancing*, features song in English but
dialogue in German. On the Reeperbahn, Pulverfass is Hamburg's
most famous *Travestie* (transvestite) show. There's plenty of
nudity and crudity and while it helps to know some German
you can get by without (expensive cover charge).

class dose of musical medicine. Check the website for events.
🄰 Grosse Freiheit 6 🕿 (040) 87 87 06 80 🅦 www.haloclubbing.de
🕓 from 23.00 Fri & Sat 🅢 S-bahn: S1, S3 to Reeperbahn

Mandarin Kasino Run by the crew who made the Mojo Club great.
Design deliberately low-key so as not to distract from the music.
🄰 Reeperbahn 1 🕿 (040) 430 46 16 🅦 www.mandarin-kasino.de
🕓 23:00 Fri & Sat, 20.00 if concert

AFTER DARK – ALTONA

Friedensallee is the place to see and be seen in Altona, with several
attractive and trendy bars. Along the waterfront, all the way to
Blankenese (see pages 124–9), are some of the city's most acclaimed,
and most expensive, gourmet restaurants. So why not take the

S-bahn to Altona, have a drink or two there, then catch a taxi to a riverside restaurant?

RESTAURANTS

Eisenstein ££ ❸ A former factory with bare stone walls and a high ceiling is the setting for this fashionable restaurant in front of the Zeisse-Kino cinema. Good pizzas served here. **ⓐ** Friedensallee 9 **ⓣ** (040) 390 46 06 **Ⓦ** www.restaurant-eisenstein.de **Ⓛ** 11.00–01.30 Mon–Sat, 10.00–01.30 Sun **Ⓝ** S-bahn: S1, S3, S31 to Altona

Clasenhof £££ ❹ Fine dining in a converted factory, with an open kitchen so you can watch your food being prepared. Relaxed and friendly atmosphere, the art on the walls is by local artists. **ⓐ** Grosse Brunnenstrasse 61a **ⓣ** (040) 280 76 98 **ⓕ** (040) 398 061 26 **Ⓦ** www.clasenhof.de **Ⓛ** 18.00–23.00 Tues–Sun, closed Mon **Ⓝ** S-bahn: S1, S3, S31 to Altona

Landhaus Scherrer £££ ❺ This Michelin-starred establishment is one of Hamburg's most famous and most acclaimed restaurants. For most people the main dining room is affordable for special occasions only but the attached Ö1 bistro is slightly less damaging to the wallet and the food is still wonderful. The building goes back to 1827 and is decorated with contemporary art. Oenophiles might like to note that there are 640 types of wine and 12,000 bottles here! **ⓐ** Elbchaussee 130 **ⓣ** (040) 880 13 25 **Ⓦ** www.landhausscherrer.de **Ⓛ** 12.00–15.00 (14.30 last orders), 18.30–23.00 Mon–Sat **Ⓝ** S-bahn: Altona

Tafelhaus £££ ❻ Modern restaurant with a beautiful summer terrace on which to enjoy some of the city's finest food. The chef's

Austrian, the cuisine is mostly German and Mediterranean with Oriental touches but don't be surprised to find Swiss, French and other influences too. ⓐ Neumühlen 17 ⓣ 89 27 60 ⓦ www.tafelhaus-hamburg.de ⓛ 12.00–16.00 (last orders 14.15), 19.00–24.00 Mon–Fri, 19.00–24.00 (last orders 21.30) Sat ⓥ Bus: 112 to Elbtreppe

BARS

Die Blaue Blume A typical German *Kneipe* with white candles cascading off dark tables and a lot of talking going on. Beer garden. As well as the usual fried potato pub meals, Asian food is also served. ⓐ Gerichtstrasse 49 ⓣ (040) 38 58 69 ⓛ 12.00–01.00 Mon–Fri, 17.00–01.00 Sat, 16.00–01.00 Sun ⓥ S-bahn: S1, S3 to Holstenstrasse

Filmhauskneipe Nice wine, nice food, simple wooden tables and chairs, and lots of arty folks chatting about the film they have just seen, or are about to see, at the Zeisse-Kino (films usually in German only) next door. ⓐ Friedensallee 7 ⓣ (040) 39 90 80 25 ⓛ 12.00–01.00 (last food orders 23.00) ⓥ S-Bahn: S1, S3, S31 to Altona

▶ *The best view of Lübeck's Marienkirche is from the tower of neighbouring St Petri*

Blankenese

You will need to dedicate a half-day to visit Blankenese ('blanken-ay-zer'), which is Hamburg's prettiest village and a delight in summertime.

GETTING THERE

By road

Bus 36 travels straight down the Reeperbahn, goes through Altona (though you see very little of it from the bus), follows the Elbe and arrives in Blankenese half an hour or so later. The S-Bahn knocks ten minutes off the journey time, but you should travel at least one way by bus to enjoy the river and parkland views and to see the beautiful houses that line the Millionaire's Row of the Elbschaussee.

SIGHTS & ATTRACTIONS

There are two 'sights' in Blankenese. The first is the village itself, an old fisherman's settlement set on a steep hill – a rarity in this part of the world – turned into a very desirable residential quarter in the 19th century by rich Hamburg merchants. It comprises some very pretty houses, including some which are thatched, and the whole area is lovingly tended and landscaped with several parks. The other sight is the view of the Elbe from the village.

Once you arrive in the relatively modern centre of Blankenese you should head to the riverfront (Strandweg) which is over 75 m (245 ft) below you. You have two options, either jump aboard mini-bus 48 (the stop is just a few yards away from the S-bahn station – which is also where bus 36 stops) – or you can walk. If you want to use the bus service, these little 'mountain goats' (as they are known

⬤ *Blankenese, Hamburg's village on a hill*

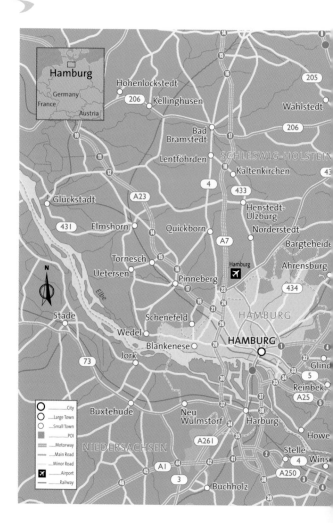

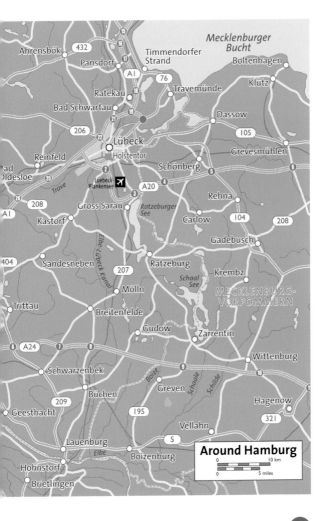

Around Hamburg

0   10 km
0   5 miles

locally) shuttle constantly between the station and river, so you won't have long to wait for one. You'll see more if you walk down, however, and even if you get a little lost it all adds to the adventure. It's better to walk down than up for obvious reasons so why not walk down and catch the bus up.

Follow Bahnhofstrasse south past the shops, past the church and the marketplace and you will come to the town's famed Treppenviertel (Steps or Staircase Quarter). Market days are Tuesday, Wednesday (organic market), Friday and Saturdays. There are around 4,800 steps in total, linking all the houses together, and the longest of these staircases is the Strandtreppe, which has over 160 steps.

Once at the riverfront walk down towards the lighthouse (a disappointingly prosaic structure for such a pretty place as Blankenese) and you will find a small golden beach lapped by the Elbe. In summer, or indeed almost any time when the sun shines, cafés set table and chairs outside and there's quite a seaside atmosphere.

On the bus back up get off at the Süllberg, the hill at the very top of the town. It's not that high but because it rises so steeply you get great views from here over the Elbe and the rest of Blankenese. A castle has stood guard over the Elbe at this point since 1060 and the present structure, built in the late 19th century, is now incorporated into a luxury hotel, whose terrace is open to visitors. From the Hotel Süllberg it's only a 5–10-minute walk back to the centre or there is a bus stop outside on the main road.
🔊 Bus: 36 from Mönckebergstrasse or S-bahn: S1 to Blankenese from Hbf

TAKING A BREAK

Kajüte SB12 Friendly little cheap-and-cheerful café on the front, by the lighthouse. In summer their tables spill onto the sands and this is a favourite meeting place for drinks and cheap eats, renowned for its *Bratkartoffelgerichte* (fried potato dishes). ➋ Strandweg 79, Blankenese ➊ 866 42 430 ➌ 10.00–late Mon–Sat, 12.00–21.00 Sun

Witthüs It's slightly out of the centre of the village but this idyllic thatched tearoom in the beautiful Hirsch Park is well worth the detour and a perfect end to a day in Blankenese. The food is superb quality and you won't find a nicer setting anywhere in Hamburg (or perhaps anywhere…) than their terrace. ➋ Elbchaussee 499a, Hirschpark, Mühlenberg entrance ➊ 86 01 73 ➌ www.witthues.de ➌ Café: 14.00–23.00 Mon–Sat, 10.00–23.00 Sun and hols; Restaurant: 19.00–23.00 Tues–Sun

ACCOMMODATION

Hotel Behrmann ££ Modern and comfortable small hotel, located between the beach and Treppenviertel. ➋ Elbchaussee 528 ➊ (040) 866 97 20 ➌ www.hotel-behrmann.de ➌ reservierung@hotel-behrmann.de

Hotel Süllberg £££ The hotel, the gourmet restaurant and the views are all five-star at this splendid castle-like hotel at the top of the hill. Take a coffee on the terrace and watch boats of every nation sailing up and down the Elbe. ➋ Süllbergsterrasse 12, Blankenese ➊ 866 25 20 ➌ www.suellberg-hamburg.de ➌ info@suellberg-hamburg.de

Lübeck

Lübeck is 59 km (37 miles) northeast of Hamburg. In the late Middle Ages it was one of Europe's richest cities and far more important than Hamburg. Its wealth came from its position as 'Queen of the Hanse', head of the Hanseatic League, the trading alliance of Dutch and North German cities which at its peak numbered over 160 members and controlled the highly lucrative Baltic Sea routes. When the monopoly of the Hanseatic League was broken and other routes became more important Lübeck's star waned. However, it has retained its maritime standing; today it is still the busiest German port on the Baltic Sea and a significant industrial centre (though visitors to the Old Town will see neither of these facets).

Lübeck's historic heart, the Old Town, is a small and compact island girdled by canals. Day visitors can cover its highlights on foot quite comfortably. However, if you have more than a single day there is more to see and do, including several museums and boat trips. If you are staying overnight there are plenty of good bars, restaurants and an active nightlife scene.

GETTING THERE

By rail
Trains run once an hour from Hamburg Hbf and take around 50 minutes. A single fare is €11, but a Schleswig-Holstein-Ticket for €29, valid for five adults travelling together, is worth buying to get you there and back the same day. From Lübeck Hbf it is a 15-minute walk to the centre of the Old Town.

🔺 *Lübeck is charming whatever time of year you visit*

LÜBECK REBUILT

Although Lübeck is frequently described as a beautiful, historic and unspoiled city, a quarter of it was lost to Allied bombing in 1942 and much of its old centre had to be rebuilt. Today it is on the UNESCO list as a World Heritage Site. However, not all the town was rebuilt in the old style and the main Holstenstrasse in particular is a typically ugly 1960s-style thoroughfare, complete with fast-food outlets and cheap shops.

SIGHTS & ATTRACTIONS

An der Untertrave & Mengstrasse

Here along the waterfront you will find several historic traditional sailing ships moored in front of beautiful gabled houses, many dating from the 17th century, including the Tesdorpf-Haus (on the corner with Mengstrasse), which is the town's oldest wine importer. Turn into Mengstrasse, a fine street full of historic houses, and take a look in at nos. 48–50, the Schabbelhaus (see After Dark, page 142).

Boat trips

Boat trips around Lübeck Harbour give you an excellent waterside view of the many fine houses that line the canals. In summer you might like to take an excursion to the Baltic Sea resort of Travemünde, 20 km (13 miles) north-east of Lübeck. There is a charming old town here, with many half-timbered houses and a long sandy beach. All trips depart from An der Untertrave.

Dom (Cathedral)

Lübeck's cathedral is overlooked by most day-visitors as it is at
the 'wrong' (southern) end of the Old Town, away from the other
attractions. It was built in 1230 but badly damaged in 1942 and
restoration has swept away its ancient atmosphere. In the churchyard
are two museums: the Museum für Natur und Umwelt (Museum of
Nature and the Environment) and the Völkerkundesammlung
(Folklore collection).

Dom ⓐ Mühlendamm 2-6 ❶ (0451) 747 04 ⓦ www.domzuluebeck.de
🕙 10.00–18.00 Apr–Oct; 10.00–16.00 Oct–Mar

Museum für Natur und Umwelt ⓐ Musterbahn 8 ❶ (0451) 122 41 22
ⓦ www.museenluebeck.de 🕙 09.00–17.00 Tues–Fri, 10.00–17.00 Sat
& Sun, closed Mon. Admission charge

Völkerkundesammlung ⓐ Zeughaus am Dom, Parade 10
❶ (0451) 122 43 42 ⓦ www.museenluebeck.de 🕙 10.00–17.00
Tues–Sun, closed Mon. Admission charge

Heiligen-Geist-Hospital (Hospice of the Holy Spirit)

One of the oldest social institutions in Germany, this splendid
complex is a church with a hospice attached, built by the city's
wealthy merchants in 1280. Its 14th-century church wall paintings
are some of the brightest and most important medieval examples
in northern Germany. Behind the church is a huge hall containing
little wooden *Kabäuschen* (cabins), where until the 1970s old and
infirm people were cared for. It is also worth looking below, in the
former wine cellars, now occupied by a restaurant. ⓐ Am Koberg
❶ (museum hotline) 01805 92 92 00 🕙 10.00–17.00 Apr–Sept;
10.00–16.00 Tues–Sun, Oct–Mar

Hidden courtyards

A short distance from the Heiligen-Geist-Hospital, in Glockengiesserstrasse, are two more examples of the city's long history of charitable institutions in the form of 17th-century almshouses. The Füchtings-Hof at no. 23 was built for the widows of sea captains, the Glandorp-Hof, entrance next to no. 49, for the widows of craftsmen. Each is set in an idyllic courtyard – you may enter but do heed the signs and do not go any further than you are invited.

Holstentor (Holstein Gate)

This fairy-tale twin-turreted gateway was built in 1478 when Lübeck was at its peak. It is the symbol of the city and the sheer bulk of this fortification, which once held 48 cannons, gives an idea as to Lübeck's historic importance. Today it is home to a small museum, which gives a brief introduction to the town. Immediately behind the gate is a row of elegant 16th-century gabled houses which were once Salzspeicher (salt warehouses). One of these has been converted into a shop, the rest are closed to the public.
ⓐ Holstentorplatz ⓣ (museum hotline) 01805 92 92 00
ⓦ www.museen.luebeck.de ⓛ 11.00–17.00 Thur–Sun, Jan–Mar; 10.00–18.00 Apr–Dec. Admission charge

HAPPY DAY CARD

A Lübeck Happy Day Card costs €6, or €12 for three days, and entitles you to discounted (usually half-price) admission at most museums, which means that after two to three visits the card pays for itself.

⬤ *The Marienkirche looms behind the façade of the Rathaus*

Jakobikirche (St James' Church)

'The Seafarers' Church' escaped the bombing of 1942 and is famous for its art treasures, most notably the 15th-century Brömse Altar and its beautifully preserved 14th-century wall paintings. It is also renowned for its organ music and features two 16th-century organs. In the north tower chapel the damaged lifeboat of the Pamir, which sank in 1957 with the loss of 80 (mostly young) lives, is a touching memorial to those lost at sea. ➋ Jakobikirchhof 5 ➊ (0451) 30 80 115 Ⓦ www.st-jakobi-luebeck.de ◷ 10.00–16.00 Tues–Sun, Nov–Mar; 10.00–18.00 Tues–Sun, Apr–Oct; open Mon in summer

Marienkirche (St Mary's Church)

This imposing edifice, constructed 1250–1350 and topped by twin spires soaring 125 m (410 ft) high, is one of the finest Gothic churches in the country and the third largest in all Germany. There are several highlights within, including its vaulted ceiling, the world's largest mechanical organ and its astronomical clock. The great bells, brought crashing down in 1942, remain where they fell, making a lasting impression on today's visitors as well as on the church floor,

where they lie in pieces. ⓐ Schüsselbuden 13 ❶ (0451) 773 91
🕐 10.00–17.00 Oct; 10.00–16.00 Nov–Mar; 10.00–18.00 Apr–Sept

Museum für Figurentheater (Puppet Theatre Museum)

Set in a terrace of five historic half-timbered houses, this fascinating,
colourful and often exotic collection claims to be the world's largest
puppet theatre museum. It features around 5,000 puppets and props
(including posters, stages and barrel organs) from all over the world
and has its own puppet theatre next door, though performances are
only in German. ⓐ Kolk 14 ❶ (0451) 786 26 Ⓦ www.en.tfm-luebeck.com
🕐 10.00–18.00 Mon–Wed & Fri–Sun, Apr–Oct; 11.00–17.00 Mon–Wed
& Fri–Sun, Nov–Mar. Admission charge

Rathaus (Town Hall)

This splendid, sprawling, late medieval complex was begun in
the 13th century and features arcades and spires and the town's
hallmark bands of glazed and unglazed brickwork. It is the oldest
working town hall in Germany. The two unusual huge 'portholes'
in the brick screen above the town hall were designed to let the
fierce Baltic sea wind howl through instead of blowing the wall
down. Don't miss the ornate Renaissance staircase of 1594 on the
main street running along the side of the building. Opposite is
another of the town's most famous institutions, the Niederegger
shop, museum and café (see pages 139–40). ⓐ Breite Strasse 64
❶ (0451) 122 10 05 🕐 Guided tours (German only) 11.00, 12.00, 15.00
Mon–Fri. Charge for tours

🔾 *The world of theatre in miniature at the Museum für Figurentheater*

Original
Scherenschnitt
Briefkarte

CULTURE

Lübeck has a strong artistic and literary background, and is the home town of Thomas Mann and Günter Grass, both winners of the Nobel Prize for Literature (1929 and 1999 respectively).

Buddenbrookhaus

Built in 1758, this beautiful house was the home of Johann Siegmund Mann, grandfather of the city's two famous sons, the author Thomas Mann (1875–1955) – best known for *Death in Venice* (1912) – and his less-celebrated literary brother Heinrich Mann (1871–1950). It is now a centre dedicated to their works. ❷ Mengstrasse 4 ❶ (museum hotline) 01805 92 92 00 Ⓦ www.buddenbrookhaus.de ⏱ 10.00–18.00 Apr–Oct; 11.00–17.00 Nov–Mar. Admission charge

Günter-Grass-Haus

Not just a study of Grass as an author, but also of his output as an artist and sculptor. ❷ Glockengiesserstrasse 21 Ⓦ www.guenter-grass-haus.de ⏱ 10.00–17.00 Nov–Mar; 10.00–18.00 Apr–Oct. Admission charge

Museum Behnhaus/Drägerhaus

The Behnhaus is a museum and gallery of 19th- and 20th-century paintings, crafts and sculptures; the adjacent Drägerhaus (same entrance) is a perfectly preserved 18th-century house with Biedermeier arts and crafts pieces. ❷ Königstrasse 9–11 ❶ (0451) 122 4148 ⏱ 10.00–17.00 Tues–Sun, Apr–Sept; 10.00–16.00 Tues–Sun, Oct–Mar. Admission charge

Willy-Brandt-Haus

In tribute to one of its worthiest sons, Lübeck has refurbished and converted the legal library of 1780 to a museum and archive of the politics of the 20th century. Willy Brandt spent his childhood in Lübeck, fled to Norway as a young man to escape the Nazi regime and went on to become an important and respected Bundeskanzler (head of government). This museum shows personal artefacts and political correspondence, TV interviews and photos. ❸ Königsstrasse 1 ❶ (museum hotline) 01805 92 92 00 ⓦ willy–brandt-luebeck.de ❶ 10.00–18.00

RETAIL THERAPY

Most of Lübeck's shops are on Breite Strasse and Königstrasse and are small and specialist, though there is a branch of Karstadt department store in the centre. There are several good food and drink outlets, typical Lübeck souvenirs being Lübecker Rotspon red wine and Lübecker marzipan nut loaf (to be enjoyed together!).

Christmas in Lübeck

Lübeck is famous for its Christmas Market, centring on the town hall square. The highlight of the town at this period, however, is the Heiligen-Geist-Hospital, which hosts a very popular Christmas Crafts Market, attracting crafts vendors from all over northern Germany. Many of these set up their stalls in the tiny cabins of the former hospice (see page 133). Expect to queue.

Niederegger

Choose from over 100 types of pastries and cakes and 300 kinds of marzipan confectionery (Lübeck has been the home of marzipan for

over 500 years) at the world's most famous marzipan shop. Niederegger also runs an old–fashioned Grand Salon-style café on the same premises.
ⓐ Breite Strasse 89 ⓣ (0451) 53 01 126 ⓦ www.niederegger.de
ⓛ 09.00–19.00 Mon–Fri, 09.00–18.00 Sat, 10.00–18.00 Sun

TAKING A BREAK

There are good restaurants, bars and cafés all over the town centre. Mühlenstrasse has the greatest concentration.

Im alten Zolln The fabric of the city's oldest pub goes back to at least 1589 and there's usually a cosy atmosphere, with locals and tourists rubbing shoulders. Inexpensive snacks at lunchtime and live music on several nights make this a good place to visit at any time.
ⓐ Mühlenstrasse 93–95 ⓣ (0451) 7 2395 ⓦ www.zolln.de ⓛ 12.00–late

AFTER DARK

Lübeck is a busy cultural centre with nightlife from church concerts to Irish pubs and punk bands. There are two free monthly listings magazines; *Heute Events & Kultur* (in English and German) and *Ultimo* (German only). The latter is also available online
ⓦ www.ultimo-luebeck.de

Haus der Schiffergesellschaft (House of the Sea Captains' Guild) ££
Entering this dark, atmospherically lit beamed space feels as if you have descended below deck on a 16th-century galleon. Founded in 1535 as a meeting room, it is festooned with maritime antiques and large time-worn model ships hang from the ceiling. It is nearly always busy and it's best to get a table well away from the doors as

◑ *Lübeck, beautiful by night*

curious visitors are constantly looking in. Despite being a tourist attraction in its own right the food is good quality and the menu specialises in fish. ⓐ Breite Strasse 2 ❶ (0451) 76 776 ⓦ www.schiffergesellschaft.de ⓛ 10.00–24.00 Tues–Sun

Schabbelhaus £££ Imagine you are an upper-class Hanseatic merchant in the grand, antiques-filled interior of this beautifully preserved 16th/17th-century house. Excellent regional cuisine and the lunchtime fixed-price menu is a bargain. ⓐ Mengstrasse 48–52 ❶ (0451) 720 11 ⓦ www.schabbelhaus.de ⓛ 12.00–14.30, 18.00–23.00 Mon–Sat

ACCOMODATION

Jugendherberge Altstadt £ Hostel in a merchant's house dating back to 1761. Five single and sixteen double rooms available. Open to members of the International Youth Hostel Federation only. ⓐ Mengstrasse 33 ❶ (0451) 702 03 99 ❶ (0451) 770 12 ⓦ www.djh.de

Klassik Altstadt Hotel ££ Privately-run hotel in historic town house and former smithy. Each of the 28 rooms is dedicated to a literary figure or artist with Lübeck connections. ⓐ Fischergrube 2 ❶ (0451) 70 29 80 ⓦ www.klassik-altstadt-hotel.de ⓔ info@klassik-altstadt-hotel.de

Radisson SAS Senator Hotel £££ Conveniently situated for the Altstadt, top comfort hotel with all amenities. ⓐ Willy-Brandt-Allee 6 ❶ (0451) 1420 ⓦ www.senatorhotel.de ⓔ info.luebeck@radissonsas.com

⬤ *After eight centuries, Hamburg continues to welcome ships of all nations*

PRACTICAL
information

Directory

GETTING THERE
By air

You can fly direct to Hamburg from all London airports and most major provincial airports in the UK. Flight time is around two hours. The cheapest flights are often provided by German Wings (from Gatwick) and Easyjet (from Bristol). British Airways and KLM provide scheduled flights. Ryanair flies to Lübeck from Stansted.

Hamburg Airport also welcomes direct flights from New York and Toronto (flight time around nine hours), as well as from most European areas. Connecting flights to and from Frankfurt Airport (and further long-distance flights) take about one hour.

Package breaks may be worth considering if you want 4- or 5-star luxury, as accommodation in Hamburg's top hotels can be expensive. If you are happy with booking your own 2- or 3-star hotel and you can get a cheap flight, however, a package is unlikely to offer you a saving. The tourist board offer a number of Happy Hamburg packages, visit Ⓦ www.hamburg-tourism.de for details.

British Airways Ⓦ www.ba.com

Easyjet Ⓦ www.easyjet.co.uk

German Wings Ⓦ www.germanwings.com

KLM Ⓦ www.klm.com

Ryanair Ⓦ www.ryanair.co.uk

Many people are aware that air travel emits CO_2, which contributes to climate change. You may be interested in the possibility of lessening the environmental impact of your flight through Climate Care, which offsets your CO_2 emissions by funding environmental projects around the world. Visit Ⓦ www.climatecare.org.

By rail

There is no direct rail link between the UK and Hamburg. Journeys involve a Eurostar trip from London St Pancras International to Paris or Brussels. If you do not want to travel overnight you will have to change at Brussels and Cologne; if you do take an overnight train then you can change at either Paris or Brussels. The standard rail fare is much more expensive than the no-frills airfare.

Eurostar Reservations (UK) ☎ 08705 186186 ⓦ www.eurostar.com

Thomas Cook European Rail Timetable ☎ (UK) 01733 416477; (USA) 1 800 322 3834 ⓦ www.thomascookpublishing.com

By road

The bus station is called ZOB (Zentraler Omnibus Bahnhof) and is just over the road from the main railway station and next-door to the Museum für Kunst und Gewerbe. Although coach services extend throughout Europe from the South of France to Scandinavia, the majority of connections are to and from Eastern Europe. There is no direct connection from London (Victoria) to Hamburg, only via Hannover, adding another two hours to a 15-hour journey. Coaches from here meet flights at Lübeck Airport (see pages 48–9). There are also around ten coaches a day between Berlin and Hamburg.

If you want to drive, DFDS Seaways operates a car ferry from Harwich to Esbjerg in Denmark, approximately 272 km (169 miles) from Hamburg. The boat departs at Harwich at 18.00 and arrives in Esbjerg at 13.00 the next day.

DFDS Seaways ⓦ www.dfdsseaways.co.uk

ENTRY FORMALITIES

Visas are not required by citizens of the USA, Canada, Republic of Ireland, Australia, New Zealand, the UK and members of other EU countries for visits of less than three months. South African nationals do require a visa. Citizens of the UK and of all countries except other EU states require a valid passport. EU citizens travelling without a passport need only a national identity card. It is recommended that you always carry a passport anyway.

There are no customs controls at borders for visitors from EU countries. Visitors from EU countries can bring in, or take out, goods without any restrictions on quantity or value, as long as these goods are for personal use only. Visitors from outside the EU are subject to the following restrictions. Most personal effects and the following items are duty-free: a portable typewriter; one video camera or two still cameras with ten rolls of film each; a portable radio, a tape recorder, and a laptop computer, provided they show signs of use; 400 cigarettes or 50 cigars or 250 g (9 oz) of tobacco; 2 litres (0.52 gallons) of wine or 1 litre (0.26 gallons) of liquor per person over 17 years old; fishing gear; one bicycle; skis; tennis or squash racquets; and golf clubs.

As entry requirements and customs regulations are subject to change, you should always check the current situation with your local travel agent, airline or a German embassy or consulate before you leave. For current information on visas and customs requirements contact: **German Department of Foreign Affairs (Auswärtiges Amt)**: Ⓦ www.auswaertiges-amt.de

MONEY

The euro (€) is the official currency in Germany. €1 = 100 cents. It comes in notes of €5, €10, €20, €50, €100, €200 and €500. Coins are in denominations of €1 and €2, and 1, 2, 5, 10, 20 and 50 cents. *Geldautomat* (ATM) machines pop up everywhere and have instructions in English. Supermarkets and many smaller businesses, including some restaurants, bars and small hotels may not accept credit cards. Travellers' cheques can be cashed at a *Wechselbüro* (exchange bureau); many banks won't change them. Banks close for lunch and opening times can vary.

HEALTH, SAFETY & CRIME
The standard of food and drink hygiene is as high – if not higher – than anywhere in northern Europe and visitors should have no problems. Likewise, the quality of healthcare and paramedical aid befits one of Europe's wealthiest cities. You must of course make sure you are insured against illness and accident before travelling, to avoid hefty bills.

Thanks to a reciprocal healthcare agreement, nationals of EU countries and some other countries can get reduced-price, sometimes free, medical treatment in Germany on presentation of a valid European Health Insurance Card (EHIC), the replacement for the previous E111 form. This card gives access to state-provided medical treatment only. Apply online (Ⓦ www.dh.gov.uk/travellers) for an EHIC and allow at least 2–3 weeks until you receive the card. On top of this, private medical insurance is still advised and is essential for non-EU visitors. Dental treatment is not available free of charge.

Crimes against tourists in Hamburg are rare and problems are usually confined to the backstreets of the red-light district (see page 110).

OPENING HOURS
Most museums and galleries are closed on Monday and open 10.00–18.00 from Tuesday to Sunday. Traditional shop opening hours are 09.00/10.00–20.00 Monday to Saturday. Most shops extend their opening hours in the four weeks preceding Christmas. Most supermarkets are open 07.00–22.00 Monday to Saturday, but Sunday shopping is only possible at bakeries.

Office hours are traditionally 07.00–16.00 Monday to Friday. Restaurants open from around 12.00 to 15.00 for lunch and

19.00–23.00 for dinner. Bars often have no set closing hours, though 04.00 is the latest that most are permitted to stay open.

TOILETS

Public toilets are not that common, but where you do find them they are generally well kept.

CHILDREN

Hamburg has lots to offer children, such as the Christmas markets (see page 11), or the fireworks at the Dom fair (see pages 110–12). The Speicherstadt is great, with the Miniatur Wunderland model railway world or the Hamburg Dungeon (see pages 91–2), and most museums have child-focussed features. To the south of Hamburg, the **Freilichtmuseum am Kiekeberg** is a museum village with all sorts of historical and agricultural activities (🅐 Am Kiekeberg 1, Harburg ① (040) 790 17 60 🕒 09.00–17.00 Tues–Fri, 10.00–18.00 Sat & Sun, Mar–Oct; 10.00–16.00 Tues–Sun, Nov–Feb 🅝 S-bahn: S3, S31 to Neugraben, then Bus: 340 to Am Kiekeberg). You can always pay a visit to the zoo (see page 101) or play in Planten un Blomen park (see pages 104–5) and try out its skating rink. In the summer you could go to the beaches at Övelgönne or Blankenese (see pages 124–9), or take a trip to the seaside resort of Travemünde, not far from Lübeck (see page 132). Children under six travel free on public transport.

Nappies and jars of organic baby food are available from most supermarkets and drugstores (all German baby food is organic), but you cannot get rusks. Germans tend to use suppositories for young children, so bring a sachet of Calpol from home for emergencies. Nearly all restaurants have a selection of smaller meals for children (*Kinderkarte*) and toddlers are often presented with a colouring book or small toy to keep them amused until their food comes.

🔺 *Treat the kids to a night at the Dom*

COMMUNICATION
Internet
Internet access points are widespread, with several internet cafés around the centre of town and may of the trendier bars and cafés offering Wi-Fi.

Phone

Coin-operated public phones are rare; far more common are card-operated phones. Telephone cards (*Telefonkarten*) can be bought at any post office and some shops such as bookshops or kiosks at railway stations. A display shows how much credit is left. Instructions on how to use public telephones are written in English in phone booths for international calls. Otherwise, lift up the receiver, insert the telephone card and dial the number.

When making an international call, dial the international code you require and drop the initial zero of the area code you are ringing. The international dialling code for calls from Germany to Australia is 0061, to the UK 0044, to the Irish Republic 00353, to South Africa 0027, to New Zealand 0064, and to the USA and Canada 001.

The code for dialling to Germany from abroad, after the access code (00 in most countries) is 49. To call Hamburg from abroad, the code is 49 40.

To call Hamburg from within Germany dial 040 and then the number, unless calling from Hamburg itself, when there is no need to dial 040. In this book, numbers in the Hamburg area are given with the area code; Hamburg telephone numbers range from 6 to 8 digits. All numbers outside Hamburg have been quoted with the area code in brackets, e.g. (0451) for a Lübeck number.

Post

Postal services are quick and efficient. Stamps can be purchased from most places that sell postcards and from post offices. The main post office is opposite the Hauptbahnhof, Kirchenallee exit. Post boxes are yellow. It costs 65 cents to send a postcard from Germany to the UK.

ELECTRICITY

The supply nationally is 220 volts (AC), 50 Hertz. Round-ended, two-pronged adapters are needed for UK and North American appliances; the latter will also need a transformer for the voltage difference.

TRAVELLERS WITH DISABILITIES

Although all trains are designed for wheelchair users, not all stations have lifts, so check the transport map before travelling. A marked section of each platform is slightly elevated to allow easier access to the carriage. All city buses have wheelchair ramps. Pedestrian crossings are equipped with audio signals for the visually impaired and the modern lifts in the stations have all signs repeated in braille.The police emergency number for people with impaired hearing is ☎ (040) 19246. The Hamburg tourist office website is an excellent source of useful information (Ⓦ www.hamburg-tourism.de). For information in your own country, contact:

Access-able Ⓦ www.access-able.com

Australian Council for Rehabilitation of the Disabled (ACROD)
⊙ PO Box 60, Curtin, ACT 2605; Suite 103, 1st Floor, 1–5 Commercial Road, Kings Grove, 2208 ☎ 02 6282 4333 Ⓦ www.acrod.org.au

Disabled Persons Assembly For New Zealand-based travellers.
⊙ 4/173–175 Victoria Street, Wellington, New Zealand ☎ 04 801 9100 Ⓦ www.dpa.org.nz

Holiday Care UK-based advice. ☎ 0845 124 9971 Ⓦ www.holidaycare.org.uk

Irish Wheelchair Association ⊙ Blackheath Drive, Clontarf, Dublin 3 ☎ 01 818 6400 Ⓦ www.iwa.ie

Society for Accessible Travel & Hospitality (SATH) For North American-based travellers. ⊙ 347 5th Avenue, New York, NY 10016, USA ☎ 212 447 7284 Ⓦ www.sath.org

Tripscope Another useful source for UK travellers. ⓐ Alexandra House, Albany Road, Brentford, Middlesex TW8 0NE ❶ 0845 758 5641 ⓦ www.tripscope.org.uk

TOURIST INFORMATION
Hamburg Tourism
Main office ⓐ Hauptbahnhof (main railway station), at the back of the station, Kirchenallee entrance. ❶ 08.00–21.00 Mon–Sat, 10.00–18.00 Sun & public holidays

There is a dedicated visitor telephone number (❶ 300 51 300, available 08.00–20.00) that deals with hotel reservations, tickets for events, package tours as well as general enquiries. See also the excellent ⓦ www.hamburg-tourism.de

Other tourist offices:
Airport ⓐ Terminal 1 and 2, Arrivals area ❶ 05.30–23.00
CCH Ticket Office Dammtor Station ⓐ Dag-Hammerskjöld-Platz ❶ 08.00–19.45 Mon–Fri, 10.00–16.00 Sat
Alster Lounge, Jungfernstieg Station ⓐ Jungfernstieg ❶ 09.00–18.30 Sun–Fri, Apr–Oct; 10.00–18.00 Sun–Fri, Nov–Mar; 10.00–16.00 Sat all year
Lübeck Tourist Office ⓐ Holstentorplatz 1 ❶ 01805 88 22 33 ⓦ www.luebeck-tourismus.de ❶ 09.30–18.00 Mon–Fri, 10.00–15.00 Sat, 10.00–14.00 Sun & public holidays, Jan–May, Oct & Nov; 09.30–19.00 Mon–Fri, 10.00–15.00 Sat, 10.00 –14.00 Sun & public holidays, Jun–Sept & Dec
St Pauli Landungsbrücken ⓐ Landungsbrücken, between piers 4 and 5 ❶ 10.00–18.00 Mon, Wed & Sun, 10.00–19.00 Tues & Thur–Sat, Nov–Mar; 08.00–18.00 Mon, Wed & Sun, 08.00–19.00 Tues & Thur–Sat, Apr–Oct

To find out what's on, pick up a free copy of the monthly English-language *Hamburg Guide* available from several hotels and shopping malls, or go on-line Ⓦ www.hamburg-guide.de

BACKGROUND READING

Buddenbrooks by Thomas Mann. Family saga starting in the bourgeois society of 19th century Lübeck, portraying the difficulties modern times bring to a prosperous Hanseatic family.

Blood Eagle by Craig Russell. A brutal criminal story set in contemporary Hamburg – lots of local colour and (place)name-dropping.

Destined To Witness: Growing Up Black in Nazi Germany by Hans. J. Massaquoi. Far easier to read than its title suggests, this book provides background information on life in Hamburg between the wars.

The Invention of Curried Sausage by Uwe Timm. A delightful read delving into memories of wartime Hamburg and culinary survival!

Hamburg: Building for the Growing City. A Guide to Architecture edited by the Free and Hanseatic City of Hamburg State Ministry for Urban Development and Environment (BSU). A compact little book detailing 100 contemporary building projects all over Hamburg. Precise descriptions accompanied by interesting photos, plus introductory information on Hamburg's various districts.

Emergencies

EMERGENCY NUMBERS
Fire service (*Feuerwehr*) ☎ 112
Emergency doctor, ambulance (*Notarzt*) ☎ 112
Police (*Polizei*) ☎ 110

MEDICAL SERVICES
If you need a doctor or dentist, check the local phone book under *Ärtzte* (doctors) or *Zahnärzte* (dentists). Consulates usually have lists of English-speaking doctors and dentists. Highstreet painkillers can only be bought from chemists.

Hospitals (*Krankenhäuser*) with emergency departments
UKE University Hospital (also for emergency dental treatment)
🚉 Martinistrasse 52 ☎ (040) 42 80 30 🚌 Bus: 20 to UKE

Pharmacies (*Apotheken*)
Pharmacies have green cross signs and pharmacists are qualified to offer medical advice on minor health problems. Addresses are listed at 🌐 www.hamburg.de.

POLICE
The following police stations (as well as police at the airport) are those most relevant for tourists visiting Hamburg:
For the city centre: Steindamm 82, just round the corner from the main station ☎ (040) 428 65-1110 🚇 all lines to Hauptbahnhof
For the Reeperbahn area: Davidwache (Hamburg's most famous police station!) Spielbudenplatz 31 ☎ (040) 428 65-1510 🚇 S-bahn: S1, S3 to Reeperbahn

For Schanzenviertel: Lerchenstrasse 82 🕿 040) 428 65-1610
🄽 U-bahn: U3 to Feldstrasse

EMBASSIES & CONSULATES

Australian Embassy 🄰 Wallstrasse 76–79, Berlin 🕿 (030) 88 00 880
🆆 www.australian-embassy.de

British Embassy 🄰 Wilhelmstrasse 70/71, Berlin 🕿 (030) 20457 0

Canadian Consulate 🄰 Ballindamm 35 🕿 (040) 46 00 270
🆆 www.berlin.gc.ca

Embassy of Ireland 🄰 Friedrichstrasse 200, Berlin 🕿 (030) 220 720
🆆 www.botschaft-irland.de

New Zealand Embassy 🄰 Atrium, Friedrichstrasse 60, Berlin
🕿 (030) 206210 🆆 www.nzembassy.com

South African Embassy 🄰 Tiergartenstrasse 18, Berlin
🕿 (030) 22 07 30 🆆 www.suedafrika.org

US Embassy 🄰 Clayallee 170, Berlin 🕿 (030) 832 9233, emergencies
only (030) 83050 🆆 www.germany.usembassy.gov

EMERGENCY PHRASES

Help!	**Fire!**	**Stop!**
Hilfe!	Feuer!	Halt!
Heelfe!	*Foyer!*	*Halt!*

Call an ambulance/a doctor/the police/the fire service!
Rufen Sie bitte einen Krankenwagen/einen Arzt/die Polizei/
die Feuerwehr!
*Roofen zee bitter inen krankenvaagen/inen artst/dee politsye/
dee foyervair!*

WHAT'S IN YOUR GUIDEBOOK?

Independent authors Impartial up-to-date information from our travel experts who meticulously source local knowledge.

Experience Thomas Cook's 165 years in the travel industry and guidebook publishing enriches every word with expertise you can trust.

Travel know-how Contributions by thousands of staff around the globe, each one living and breathing travel.

Editors Travel-publishing professionals, pulling everything together to craft a perfect blend of words, pictures, maps and design.

You, the traveller We deliver a practical, no-nonsense approach to information, geared to how you really use it.

Editorial/project management: Lisa Plumridge
Copy editor: Paul Hines
Layout/DTP: Alison Rayner
Proofreader: Yvonne Bergman

Paul Murphy would like to thank Elif Lavas and the staff of the Hamburg Tourismus for the generous assistance that they provided with the original research for the first edition of this guidebook. Debby Mayes would like to thank Frau Doris Schütz at Lübeck Press Office.